tommy emmanuel

CGP

A Step-by-S...
Guitar Sty...

by

Cover Photo by Simone Ceccetti

ISBN 978-1-4234-7529-3

Hal•Leonard
CORPORATION

7777 W. BLUEMOUND RD. P.O. BOX 13819 MILWAUKEE, WI 53213

Visit Hal Leonard Online at
www.halleonard.com

ACKNOWLEDGMENTS

Thanks to my family—my beautiful wife Alli and my pride and joy, Lennon—for their inexhaustible patience. Thanks also to my mother, father, and sister for their continued support and encouragement through the years.

I'd like to express my gratitude to the fine folks at Hal Leonard for all the hard work that went into making this book the finished product it's become.

And, of course, thanks to Tommy Emmanuel for the beautiful music and endless source of inspiration.

THE RECORDING

Recorded and mixed by Chad Johnson at Tupperware Sounds, NC

Adam Moses: Drums
Eric Welch: Bass
Bill Stevens: Keyboards
Chad Johnson: Guitars, additional keyboards and programming

TOMMY EMMANUEL: DOWN UNDER'S BEST KEPT SECRET

There are very few players worthy of C.G.P. (**C**ertified **G**uitar **P**layer) status. As the founder of that elite club, Chet Atkins should know. And when Chet Atkins calls you "without a doubt, one of the greatest guitar players on the planet," you know you're doing something right. Tommy Emmanuel has been doing many things right for over four decades, wowing audiences of musicians and non-musicians alike throughout the world. Like fellow pickers extraordinaire Chet and Mark Knopfler, Emmanuel seems to possess that sixth sense when it comes to framing a melody on the fretboard. His arrangements never sound clunky, forced, or contrived. Instead, they afford the listener a clear channel into the heart of the music he performs.

Born in 1955 to a musical family, Tommy began playing guitar at the tender age of four. He was originally taught by his mother for the purpose of accompanying her on lap steel guitar, but it didn't take long for his own interest in the instrument to surface. Emmanuel can clearly remember the first time he ever heard Chet Atkins at the age of seven, and it had a profound impact on him. He spent countless hours trying to decipher Atkins' complex fingerstyle approach. Before he was 10 years old, he'd already earned years of experience as a professional musician traveling with his family, performing across Australia. Emmanuel played mostly rhythm guitar at this time, while his brother Phil (also an accomplished guitarist) played lead. The brothers rarely attended school until forced to do so by the Department of Education.

Tommy's father died of a heart attack when he was only 11 years old. Consequently, the Emmanuel siblings (including his brother Chris on drums and sister Virginia on slide guitar) earned the household's sole income for years. Shortly after his father's premature death, Emmanuel wrote a letter to "Mr. Guitar" (Atkins himself) and was shocked when he received correspondence back. Though it would still be years before their first meeting in person, the two grew to become friends, and Chet became Tommy's mentor. Around the age of 14, Emmanuel moved to Sydney to pursue a full-time music career of his own. He quickly found work in several bands and before long found himself in demand as one of the hottest session guitarists in town. He performed on recordings by Air Supply ("All Out of Love," "Every Woman in the World," etc.) and Men At Work, to name a few. He also lent his talents to countless commercials and T.V. shows. In 1980, Emmanuel finally made the trip to the U.S., meeting and playing with Chet for the first time. Since then, Mr. Guitar has done much to aid Emmanuel's career, for which he is eternally grateful.

Emmanuel's first solo album, *Up from Down Under*, appeared in 1987, and numerous subsequent releases enjoyed great success in his native Australia. In 1996, he recorded *The Day Fingerpickers Took Over the World* with Chet, for which he received his first Grammy nomination. Shortly thereafter, with the release of *Midnight Drive* in 1997, he began to garner the attention in the States that he'd long enjoyed in Europe, Asia, and his homeland. Since then, his popularity has continued to grow worldwide, no doubt spurred on by his performance at the 2000 Olympic Games in Sydney. He released his first solo acoustic album, *Only*, in 2001, beginning a trend that many fans have long been waiting for.

With increased exposure in the media all the time—he's a YouTube favorite—Emmanuel's fan base continues to expand like never before. Performing close to 300 dates a year, he's right where he wants to be: spreading his love for music and sharing his inimitable gift with the rest of us. Play on, Tommy.

ANGELINA
(*Endless Road*, 2004)

By Tommy Emmanuel

On *Endless Road*, Tommy was in full acoustic mode, concentrating all of his formidable efforts on the solo genre. The results are truly astonishing. The intro alone to his reworking of "Somewhere Over the Rainbow" is nothing short of breathtaking. Among the many gems is "Angelina," a beautiful, timeless Emmanuel original filled with many pleasant twists and turns throughout.

Figure 1—Sections A (Intro) and B (Theme)

Note: Emmanuel fingers this song in the key of D, but the capo on the second fret causes the song to sound in the key of E. For simplicity, the following analysis will be in D, and all pitch references will be in relation to the guitar key—not sounding pitch.

Tommy plays "Angelina" in drop D tuning, making full use of the deep, rich tone afforded by the slackened bass string, and uses a hybrid picking technique as opposed to all fingers. The eight-measure intro A sets up the key with a I–IV–V progression (D–G–A) of arpeggios and the occasional finger-strummed chord (measure 4). The top note of each arpeggio forms a syncopated melody of E–C♯–B–A, which lay in contrary motion to the rising D–F♯–G–A bass line.

The main theme B begins with the same three pickup notes as the intro (A–D–E), each played on a separate string so they're allowed to ring together. In fact, the first 1 1/2 measures of section A are very similar to the intro, using the same bass line and rhythmic timing of the melody, though the melody notes have changed. Halfway through measure 10, however, with the F♯7/A♯ *secondary dominant* (V of vi), it's clear that we're headed in a different direction. What follows in measures 11–26 is a modal-mixing, kaleidoscopic swirl of harmonic color. Emmanuel's groove is relaxed yet rock-solid throughout, despite the inclusion of quarter-note triplets (measures 11 and 19), harmonized melody in 6ths (measures 13–14), all kinds of grace-note hammers, pulls, and slides, and more syncopations than you can shake a stick at.

The B section is arranged at first in four-measure phrases, each one beginning with the I (D)–iii (F♯m)–IV (G)–III (F♯7/A♯) progression but ending differently in antecedent and consequent format. The first phrase ending, used in measures 11–12 and 19–20, spirals through the harmonic rollercoaster ride of vi (Bm)–♭VII (Csus2)–♭III (F6)–II7 (E7)–V7 (A7sus4). The second phrase ending, used in measures 15–16, is much tamer, stepping through V (A)–II7 (E7)–V (G/A and A). At measure 21, the fourth repetition of the phrase begins but quickly steers off course with a step-wise progression (I–ii–iii–IV), heading for the delayed resolution on D in measure 25 by way of a IV (Gmaj7)–♭IIImaj7 (Fmaj7)–IV7 (G7) detour in measure 24. Emmanuel decorates the end of the section with ornamental hammer-ons and pull-offs around the tonic chord.

Fig. 1

Gtr. 1: Drop D tuning, capo II:
(low to high) D–A–D–G–B–E

Moderately ♩ = 125

1 — Full Band

2 — Slow Demos
Gtr. 1 meas. 9-16, 21-26

Gtr. 1 (acous.)

Emaj7 (Dmaj7) · E6/G♯ (D6/F♯) · Aadd9 (Gadd9) · Bsus4 (Asus4) · Emaj7 (Dmaj7) · E6/G♯ (D6/F♯)

mf
w/ pick & fingers
let ring throughout

* Symbols in parentheses represent chord names respective to capoed guitar.
Symbols above reflect actual sounding chords. Capoed fret is "0" in tab. Chord symbols reflect implied harmony.

Figure 2—Section [C] (Bridge)

For the bridge (section [C]), Emmanuel begins on the vi chord and, for the most part, opens up the texture so that there's less going on all at once. Things are happening more in tandem here; the melody will stand alone for a few beats (measures 1, 3, 8, etc.), the bass line will take the reigns for a few (measure 4), or some chord punches will take center stage (measure 6). That's not to say that any of this is easy—and it's certainly not as easy as Emmanuel makes it sound—but things aren't quite as crowded here, which makes for a beautiful contrast to section [A]. Notice the chromatically descending bass line created by the first three chords: Bm–F#7#5/A#–D/A. This is one of Emmanuel's favorite devices and can also be heard in "Since We Met" (also in this volume), among others. The deliberately all-picked melody at the beginning of measure 5 makes a nice, subtle statement, as do the three consecutive triads at the end of measure 6.

The first phrase, which lasts from measures 1–8, repeats for the most part in measures 9–14. At measure 15, though, Emmanuel begins to do what he does best: delaying the resolution to the tonic chord. After E7 and E11 in measures 15 and 16, respectively, he really yanks on the ear with a Dm/A—the *minor* version of the tonic chord—though this is diffused somewhat by the Aadd9 that quickly follows. What closes the section is a thing of pure beauty: after three seventh-fret harmonic "pickup notes," Emmanuel blends fretted notes and ringing open strings to cascade down a D major scale (measure 18) before finishing off with a graceful legato melody that leads seamlessly back into a repeat of the main theme.

Performance Tip: Be sure to keep your fingers arched in measure 18 so that the open strings are allowed to fully ring out. That's the key to the harp-like sound achieved here.

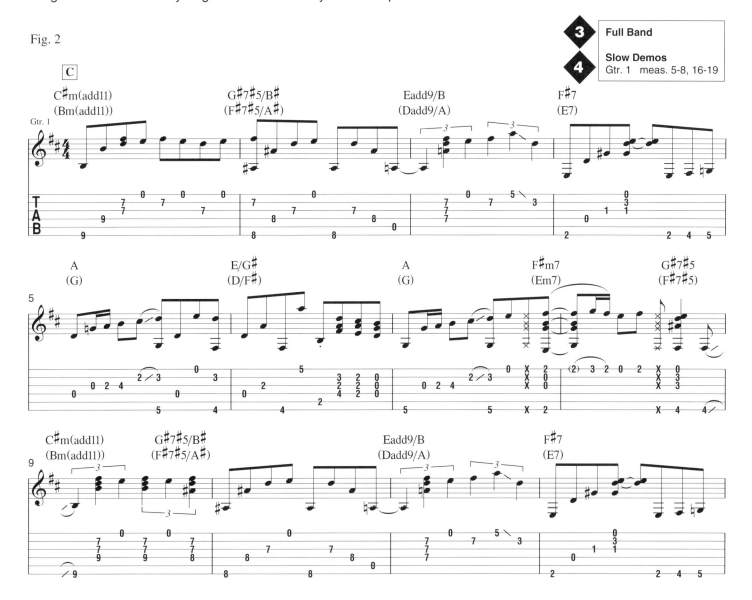

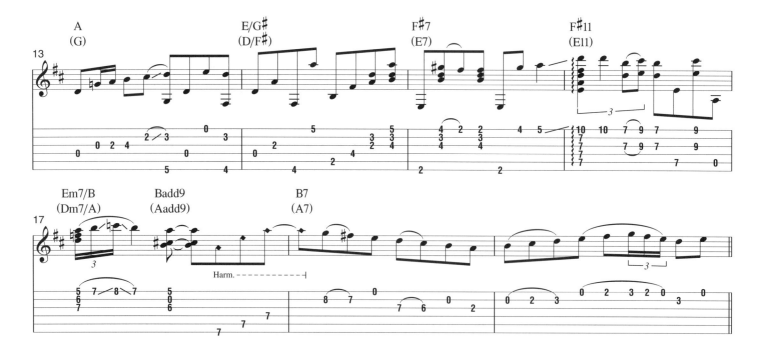

Figure 3—Section D (Coda)

This section is very short, but it's simply too striking not to include here. In a display that would make Eddie Van Halen eat his heart out, Emmanuel chimes his way through a pristine, bell-like melody, mixing twelfth-, seventh-, and fifth-fret natural harmonics with fretted notes to close out the tune in style.

Performance Tip: In order to make the harmonics really sound clearly, pick a little closer to the bridge than normal and quickly lift those fret-hand fingers off after picking the string!

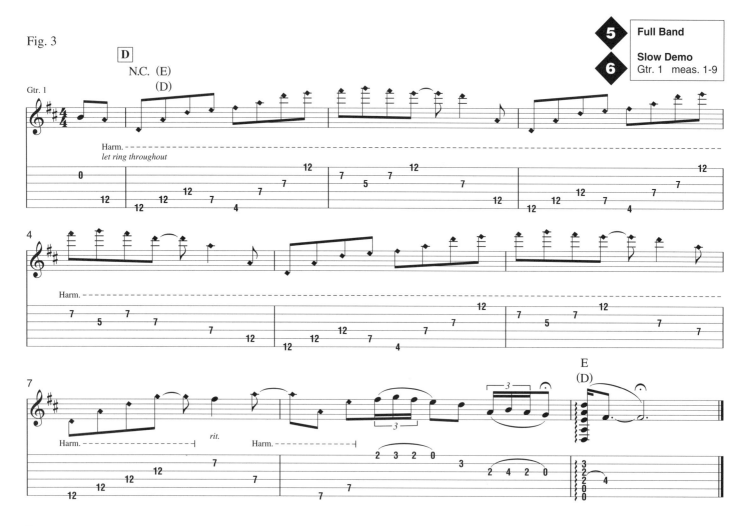

CAN'T GET ENOUGH
(*Can't Get Enough*, 1996)

By Tommy Emmanuel and Randy Goodrum

Released in 1996, *Can't Get Enough* is a full-band album on which the acoustic guitar usually takes center stage. Complimented with guest appearances by Emmanuel's idol Chet Atkins and guitar legends Larry Carlton and Robben Ford, the highly polished tracks mostly tread along the smooth jazz/light funk road and provide a rich harmonic palette over which Emmanuel can strut his stuff. On the title track, Tommy gives some love to both acoustic and electric guitars.

Figure 4—Sections A (Intro) and B (Theme)

Over the eight-measure intro (section A), the light, funky groove is established with the I–♭VI–V progression that supports the main theme (section B): G9–E♭maj7–D11. Emmanuel decorates the section with sparse, well-placed licks on acoustic (Gtr. 2) derived mostly from the G *composite blues scale* (G–A–B♭–B–C–D♭–D–E–F), which can be thought of as a combination of G major pentatonic and G blues scales. The lick in measures 4–5 is a prime example of this composite approach, as Emmanuel makes use of both G blues scale and major pentatonic sounds, whereas the slick run in measures 6–7 is straight G blues scale. Be sure to notice Emmanuel's articulation in the latter, however; his varied dynamic attack lends extraordinary character to what's essentially a straight descent down the scale.

For the main theme (section B), he rides atop the G9–E♭maj7–D11 progression with intelligent note placement, drawing from the G composite blues over the G9 and switching to the parallel G minor when playing over the E♭maj7. Since the E♭ chord is borrowed from the G minor mode, the accompanying G minor scale choice is perfectly suited and makes for a lyrical answer phrase.

In measure 17, we find a new diatonic four-measure progression that begins on the ii chord (Am7). Here, Emmanuel (doubled by another acoustic, Gtr. 4) uses 6ths to articulate a harmonized melody on strings 1 and 3, sticking mostly to notes from the G major scale. The section rounds out with another four-measure modal-mixing progression: Am7–Gmaj7–C/F–E♭maj7–D11. Emmanuel creates a syncopated arpeggio figure on the top three strings in which common G and A notes (on strings 2 and 1, respectively) are combined with alternating E and D notes on string 3. This riff is reminiscent of Eric Johnson and will require a bit of a left-hand stretch to pull off cleanly.

Fig. 4

7 — Full Band

8 — Slow Demos
Gtr. 2 meas. 6-7, 9-10

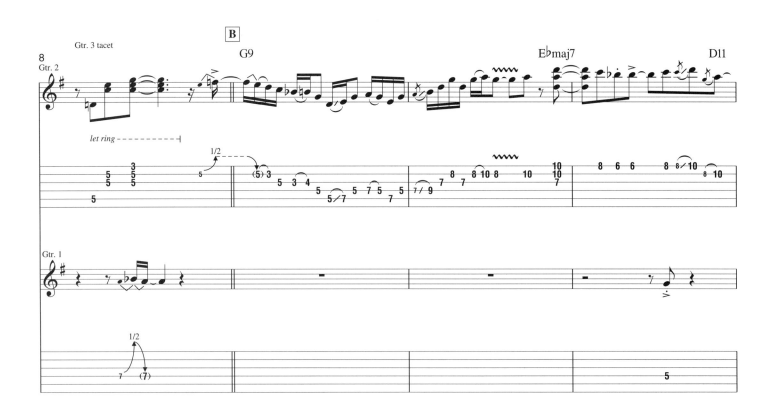

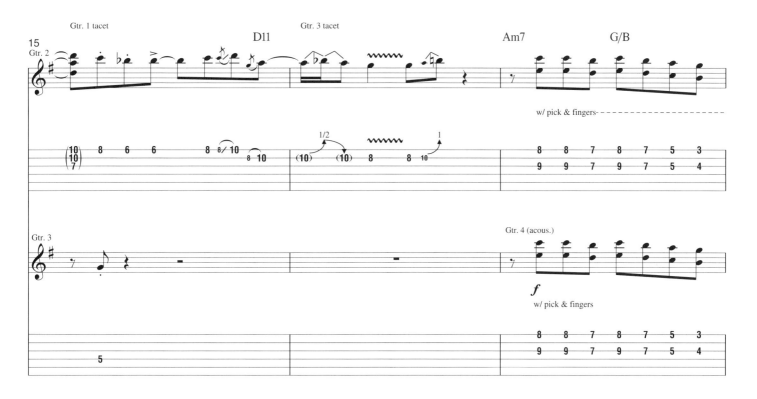

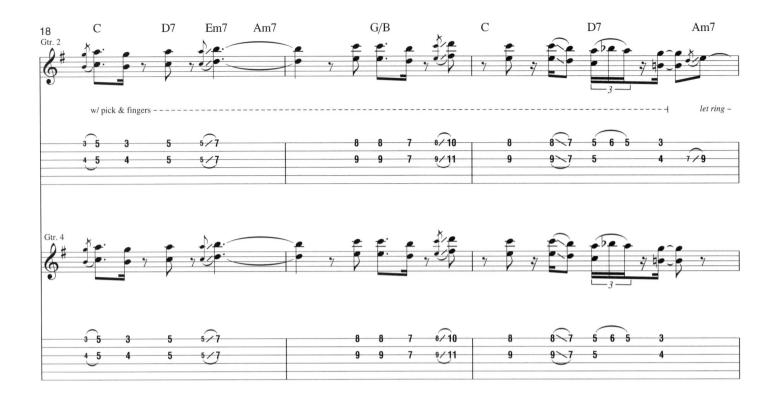

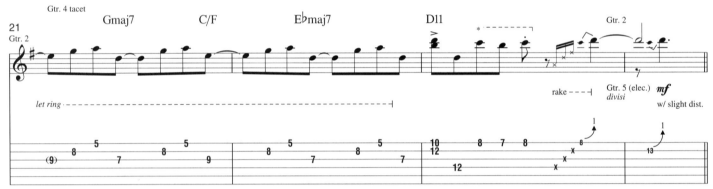

* Played behind the beat.

Figure 5—Section [C] (Bridge)

After another statement of the main theme (section B, not shown), a contrasting bridge appears containing some tricky changes. Section C is an eight-measure phrase broken into two smaller four-measure segments. The first phrase contains Cm7–F7–Bm7–E7 changes, which can be seen as a ii7–V7 in B♭ (Cm7–F7) and a ii7–V7 in A (Bm7–E7). This practice of stringing together of ii–V progressions is a staple in the jazz genre. Emmanuel navigates these jazzy waters in a chord-melody style, employing moving triads on strings 2–4 for the first two measures and an arpeggiated Bm7 voicing in measure 3.

The E7 chord in measure 4 does resolve as expected to Amaj7 in measure 5. This Amaj7 kicks off a stream of major 7th chords descending by a whole step every two beats in measures 5–6: Amaj7–Gmaj7–Fmaj7–E♭maj7. Over this tricky descent, Emmanuel moves the same triadic arpeggio figure down in whole steps, closely following the chords. The E♭maj7 chord slides via a half step down to D11, upon which Emmanuel resolves his line with the 5th (A). This D11 cleverly sets up another statement of the main theme in G (not shown). A closer look reveals that we've seen this same whole-step root-movement trick before. At the end of section B, the form rounded out with **A**m7–**G**maj7–**C/F**–**E♭**maj7–D11, lending an interesting cohesion to the tune.

Fig. 5

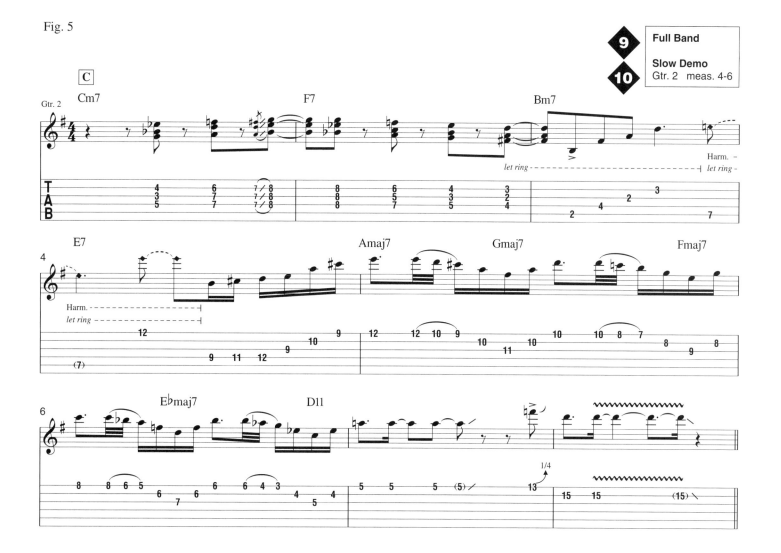

Figure 6—Section □D□ (Guitar Solo)

The guitar solo (section □D□) takes place over the exact same changes as the main theme, except that the song has modulated up a half step to A♭. The only other difference is that the V chord at the end (E♭11 in this case) has been extended by two measures to create an 18-measure form.

Tommy hands the electric over to fellow legend Larry Carlton for this solo, and Carlton tears it up with his signature smooth but biting tone. He spends most of the first eight measures camped out in the "B.B. box" at ninth position, again plucking chord-appropriate fruits from the composite blues scale tree. Noteworthy is his constant awareness of the harmony beneath him, as he carefully avoids the major 3rd (C) when playing over the F♭maj7 chord. This is made most apparent in measure 7, in which he peels off a triplet run straight out of the A♭ minor pentatonic scale and effectively highlights the major 7th (E♭) of the F♭maj7.

Measures 9–12 find Carlton stressing more of the A♭ major pentatonic side of the A♭ composite blues scale, as the chords here are all diatonic to A♭ major. He does slip in the blues/funk approved minor-to-major 3rd hammer-on in measure 12 along with some R&B-infused double-stop work in measure 10. Over the descending progression of B♭m7– A♭maj7–D♭/G♭–F♭maj7–E♭11 in measures 13–15, Carlton employs a clever melodic device known as *contrary motion*. As the root of the chords descend by whole steps, he pivots a rising scalar melody (C–D♭–E♭–F) on string 1 against the common-tone A♭ note on string 2 for dramatic effect. He returns to the composite blues scale vocabulary for the extended V chord (E♭11) that rounds out the form, bringing things to a sizzling close in measure 18 with a burning double-time lick. Note the inclusion of both minor and major 3rds (C♭ and C♮, respectively) as well as the ♭5th blue note, spelled here enharmonically as D♮.

Fig. 6

Figure 7—Section $\boxed{\text{E}}$ **(Outro)**

The outro consists of the same four-measure progression of the intro, but it's been transposed up to A (yet another half step up from the previous modulation to A♭ for the guitar solo). After rolling out four measures of a textural, sixteenth-note octave line via Gtr. 1 (acoustic), Emmanuel quickly turns the section into a headcutting contest with guest soloist Larry Carlton, trading breaks on acoustic and electric, respectively, through to the fade. The A composite blues scale does once again make up a good portion of the melodic output, but each player pulls out a few new tricks as well.

A good case in point is the charging ascent in measure 7. Over the ♭VI chord (Fmaj7), Emmanuel races up an arpeggio figure that quickly covers a two-octave span in two beats. The first two beats suggest a Dm7 sound, lending a major 13 sound to the Fmaj7 harmony. On beats 3 and 4, however, he increases the tension further by twice nicking the colorful B note—the ♯11th of Fmaj7. Also, be sure not to miss Carlton's electric line in measures 9–10, which begins in typical composite blues fashion but quickly turns heads on beat 2 of measure 10 with the inclusion of the *major* 7th (G♯) over the dominant A9 chord. This use of a major 7th over a dominant harmony is a common device in jazz, but it's much less frequently mastered by rock and blues players.

Emmanuel's lines get a bit meaner as things progress as well. In measure 16, for example, he eschews the E11 chord's A major implications and opts to plow through it with an A blues scale romp, only briefly acknowledging the major tonality with a C–C♯ hammer on the final sixteenth note. This heightened sense of reckless abandon is echoed by Carlton in measure 28 near the fade with a chromatically ascending pull-off lick on string 1, climaxing with the target E note, the 5th of the tonic A9 chord.

⑬ **Full Band**

⑭ **Slow Demos**
Gtr. 2 meas. 7-8, 16-17
Gtr. 5 meas. 9-10

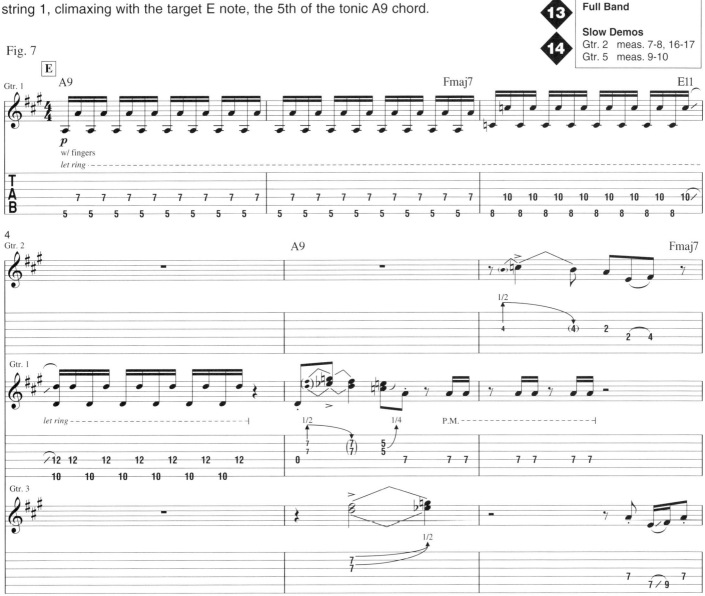

Fig. 7

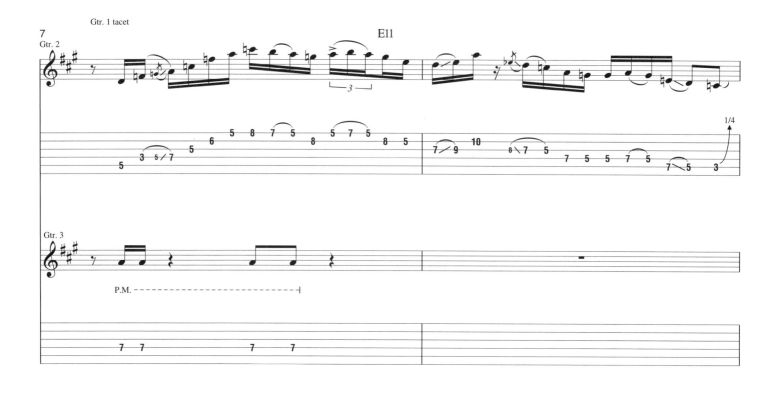

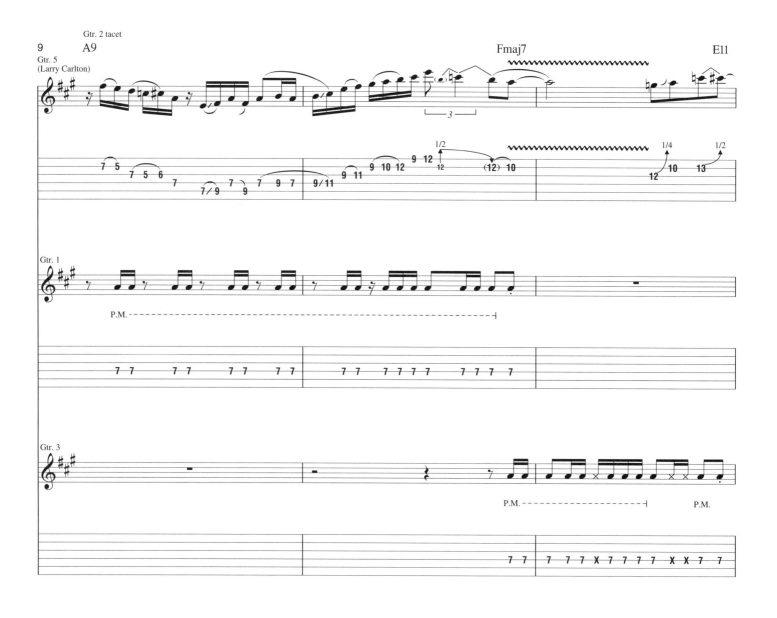

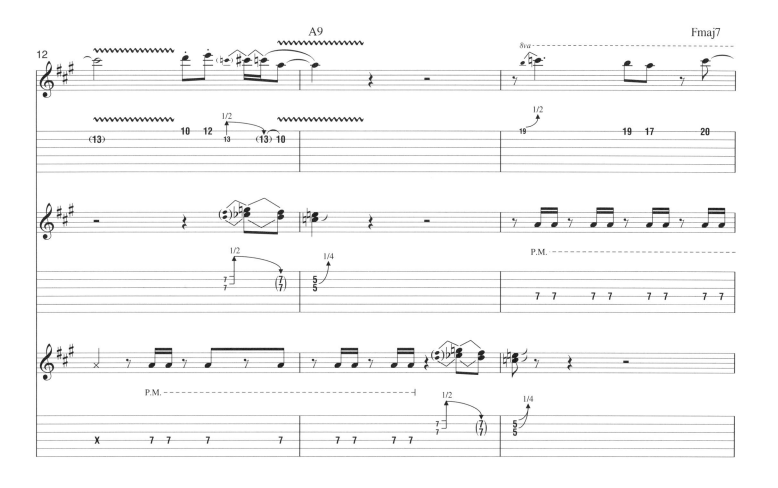

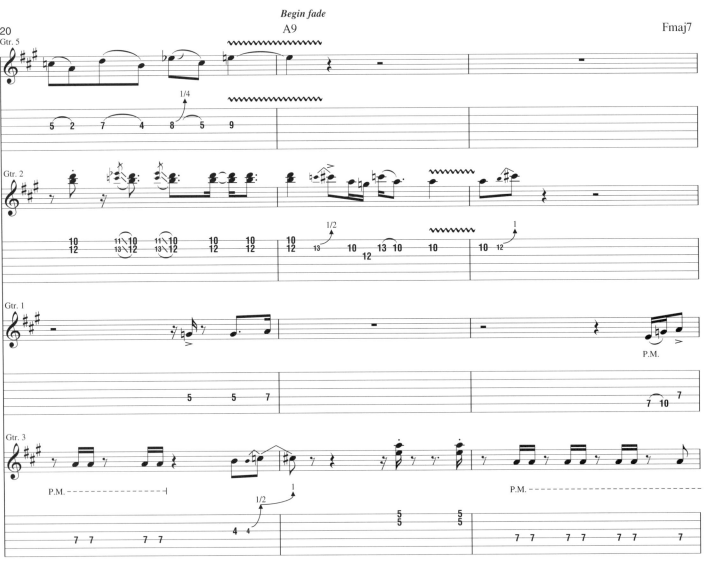

*2nd string is caught with same
finger that's bending 1st string.

COUNTRYWIDE
(*Dare to Be Different*, 1990)

By Tommy Emmanuel

On 1990's *Dare to be Different*, Emmanuel covers a fairly wide range of styles—from down and dirty boogies (see "Guitar Boogie," pg. 41) to reverb-drenched easy listening. The glue that holds the album together though is his mastery of each style. Whether navigating jazzy changes or riffing over a one-chord romp, Emmanuel's technique and taste shine through effortlessly. "Countrywide" is one of the more understated tunes of the bunch. A steady, plodding beat sets the backdrop for this tune, as T.E. adds tasteful, subtle acoustic layers of melody and harmony that lull the listener into a head-bobbing Zen-like state.

Figure 8—Sections A (Intro) and B (Theme 1)

Harmonically speaking, "Countrywide" is on the barebones side of Tommy Emmanuel. A large portion of sections A and B consist of nothing but the tonic (Am) and ♭VII (G) chords. In keeping with the title, this casts images of a lonesome, barren landscape somewhere out West. In measures 1–8, Emmanuel sets the tone of the intro by Travis picking through the chords with subtle, syncopated accents to contrast the straight, half-time feel of the band. He doubles himself throughout here on a second acoustic, playing slight variations on the pattern to create a wide blanket of sound. In true Chet fashion, he alternates between root (A) and 5th (E) bass notes on the Am chord throughout.

In measure 9, the main theme B is introduced, and Emmanuel states this with yet another overdubbed acoustic (Gtr. 3). Working out of the A minor scale in open position, he mixes arpeggios and melodic runs here, creating a part that wouldn't sound completely empty even without Gtrs. 1 & 2. In measure 17, he breaks from the two-chord vocabulary, adding C, Em, and F harmonies to the fold. Emmanuel climbs steadily as Gtr. 3 through this section, rising with a syncopated melody from the open position all the way up to the tenth-fret A on string 2 to cap off the form.

Performance Tip: The use of a thumbpick (as Tommy uses) is recommended to reproduce the crisp bass tones heard on the original recording. Also, as Tommy demonstrates when playing this tune solo, it's quite possible to create an arrangement that combines the melody of Gtr. 3 with the Travis picking of Gtrs. 1 & 2.

Fig. 8

15 Full Band

16 Slow Demos
Gtr. 1 meas. 1-4
Gtr. 3 meas. 13-15

* Chord symbols reflect implied harmony.

Figure 9—Section C (Theme 2)

For section C , the rains stop, the clouds part, and the sun comes out, which means a change in key to the parallel A major. The texture mostly stays the same here, with Emmanuel pecking out the melody on Gtr. 3 while backing himself on Gtrs. 1 & 2. After the A6 in measures 1–2, he creates some colorful harmonies via the open high E string: Badd11/A (measures 3–4), G6 (measures 5–6), and Dadd9/F♯ (measures 7–8). Take note of the way Emmanuel strums the full chords on the first beat of each to make a dramatic statement. This can be accomplished with the thumbpick or by flicking through the strings with the top side of the nails.

This eight-measure phrase begins to repeat in measure 9, but after the Badd11/A of measures 11–12, the distant thunder begins to move closer once more. Instead of the fairly innocuous G6 that occurred in the first phrase, Emmanuel moves to F6 in measure 13—a harmony much more closely tied to an A minor tonality. Indeed, in measure 15, we receive confirmation that dark clouds have come to stay, as a two-measure iim7♭5–V progression in A minor (Bm7♭5–E7) occurs twice to create an 18-measure form and heighten the dramatic return to theme 1 in A minor (not shown). Emmanuel closes off the section in measures 17–18 with a lighting bolt of a lick that descends through the A *harmonic minor scale*.

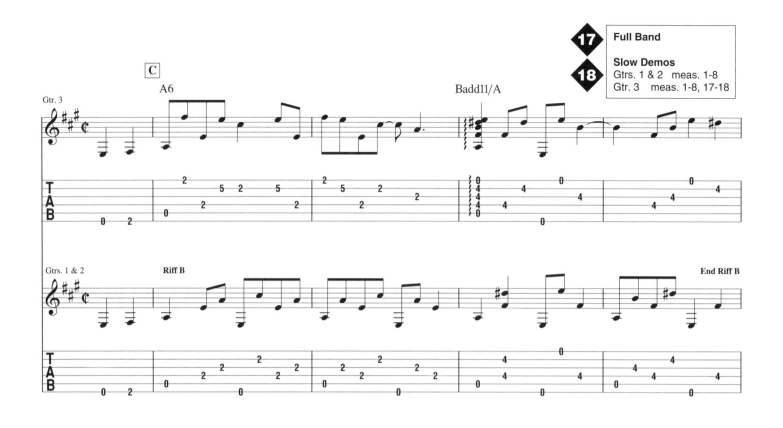

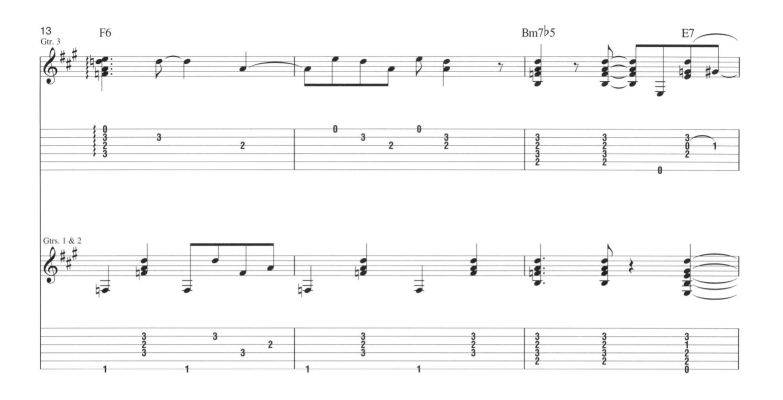

DETERMINATION
(*Determination*, 1992)
By Tommy Emmanuel

Emmanuel continued the style-hopping trend of 1990's *Dare to Be Different* with *Determination*, juggling guitar-heavy tunes with lush, heavily-produced soundscapes. He gives quite a bit of love to the Tele on many of these tunes, as was his M.O. during the earlier years. Along with the swaggering "Stevie's Blues," he seriously struts his stuff on the title track, a bouncing, funk number that basically serves as a solo vehicle.

Figure 10—Section B (Theme)

The 16-measure main theme of "Determination" takes place mostly over the bluesy changes of D7sus4 (I), G7sus4 (IV), and A7sus4 (V). However, a B♭7sus4 (♭VI) is thrown in at the end of each eight-measure section to shake things up just a bit. Tommy's tone here has a great midrange bite, and a slapback delay thickens things up considerably. Note that Gtr. 1 chinks away on the same three-note chord figure throughout all the changes. These three notes (G–C–D) coincidentally work extremely well against each harmony. As the synth and horns provide most of the harmonic backdrop, Gtr. 1's part adds more of a texture than anything.

The melody is constructed entirely from the D blues scale (D–F–G–A♭–A–C), and Emmanuel's phrasing is vocal-like throughout, consisting of as many slid and bent notes as straight ones. For the most part, the tonic (D) is targeted as a point of resolution, while the 4th (G) is briefly held for a bit of melodic tension. Notice that Emmanuel does make it a point, however, to land squarely on the A note when the V chord (A7sus4) occurs midway through the phrases in measures 4 and 12.

Performance Tip: Be sure to pay attention to the reverse slides used predominantly throughout. This technique, which is often used by Robben Ford and Larry Carlton, is largely responsible for the melody's sassy attitude.

Fig. 10

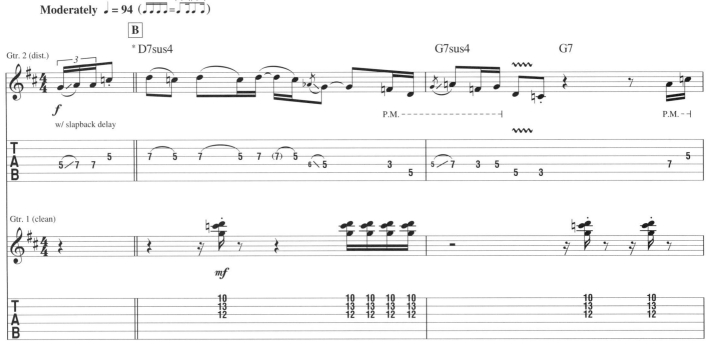

* Chord symbols reflect overall harmony.

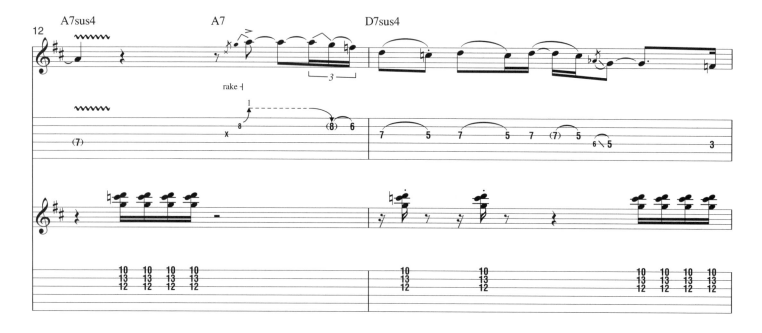

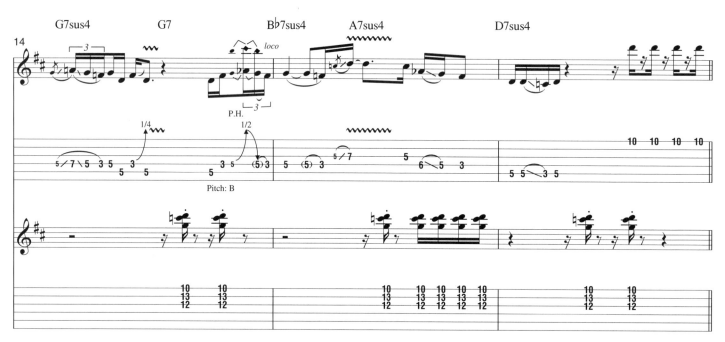

Figure 11—Section [C] (Bridge)

In section [C] , we hear a new progression that starts on the IV chord—a very common move for a bridge section. After volleying back and forth between IV (G7) and I (D7) chords three times, the section comes to a close with a V of V (E7) resolving to the V (A7), which sets up a return to the main theme (not shown). This would normally make for an eight-measure phrase, but Emmanuel extends the V chord for an extra measure (as he's prone to do), making for a nine-measure section.

To heighten the drama, Emmanuel moves up to the higher octave for this section. The "melody" here is even more loosely constructed than that of the main theme, as the only real recurring motif is the B–D hook that kicks off measures 1, 5, and 7. The spaces between are filled mostly with riffing from the D blues scale. He has broadened the melodic vocabulary a bit, though, by including sassy bends to the ♭3rd (F) from the 9th (E). Taken together with the prominent, aforementioned B notes, the scale in use can best be described as a hybrid between the D Dorian mode and blues scale—basically, a D Dorian mode with an added ♭5th (D–E–F–G–**A♭**–A–B–C).

The exception to this occurs in measure 8 over the V chord, where Emmanuel peels off a slithering, chromatically laced lick that culminates with an A blues scale run (A–C–D–E♭–E–G) in measure 9. A closer look at the chromatic lick in measure 8 reveals a method to the madness: Emmanuel is moving the same three-note chromatic fragment down in half steps each time. The first incarnation appears as A–A♭–G, starting on the "and" of beat 1. He then slides that fragment down in half steps, repeating the process four times. Combined with the chromaticism, the three-against-four syncopated rhythm makes for an especially wobbly line. This is a very effective way to turn some heads, but it's extremely important that you're able to land on your feet when you're done freefalling! Tommy, of course, has no trouble in that regard.

Fig. 11

20 Full Band

21 Slow Demos
Gtr. 2 meas. 6-9

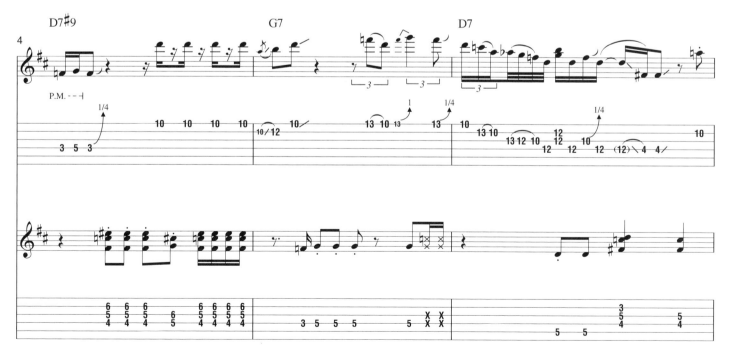

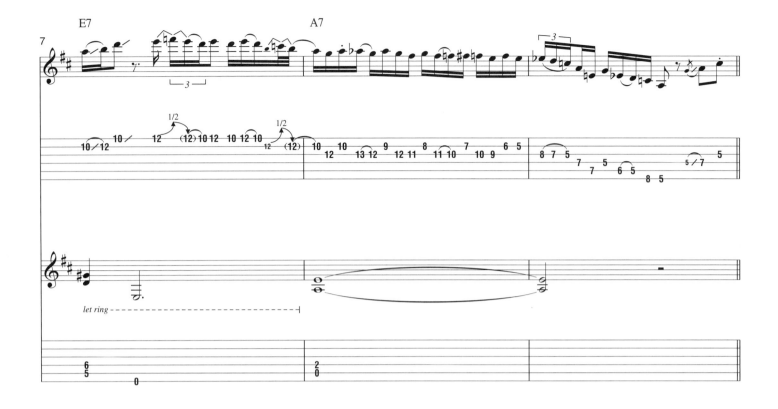

Figure 12—Sections D and E (Guitar Solo 1)

After a second statement of the main theme (not shown), the remaining sections of "Determination" kind of blend into one continuous solo. But we're going to call sections D and E guitar solo 1; this occurs from approximately 1:58 to 2:41 in the original recording. Tommy takes a break here over the main theme and bridge changes. Again, the D Dorian/blues hybrid constitutes most of his note selection, but several spots are noteworthy.

After some gusty double-stop work to kick things off, Emmanuel launches into an ascending D minor pentatonic sequence in measure 5 over D7sus4 that climaxes with a wailing bend of F to G over G7 in measure 6. Take note of the specifically placed pull-offs, which help facilitate the speed, and the slide on beat 4, which aids in the necessary position shift. Some Stevie Ray-sounding double-stop bends appear in measure 7, as do some quick, low tonic-note thumb-fretted jabs—another hallmark of the late Texas blues virtuoso.

Lending a sense of cohesion to the proceedings, Emmanuel kicks off the second section of the solo (section E) in measure 9 with the same B–D motif heard in the bridge. He bends his way through the ensuing D7 and G7 in measures 10 and 11, respectively, with some snaky phrasing that wraps itself into another tightly coiled sextuplet figure in measure 12. He strikes out with more double- and triple-stop work in measures 13–14 and reprises his B–D motif once again for the E7 in measure 15. After targeting the 3rd (C♯) of the A7 chord in measure 16 with a whole-step bend, he brings the section to a muted close with a long, sustained A note treated to a liberal amount of vibrato.

Performance Tip: For the pivoting, organ-style double-stop licks of measures 7 and 14, a hybrid picking technique (i.e., the use of both pick and fingers) will likely serve you best.

Fig. 12

D **Guitar Solo 1**

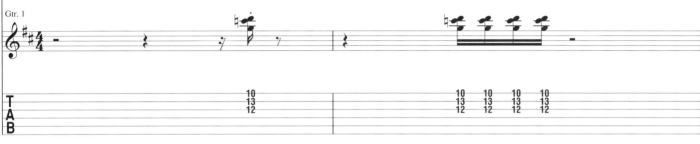

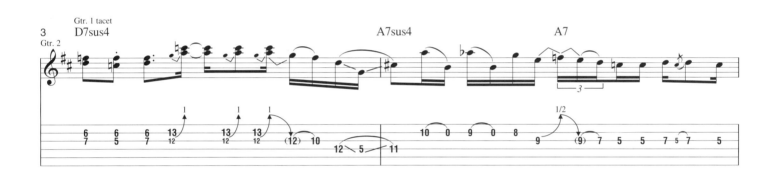

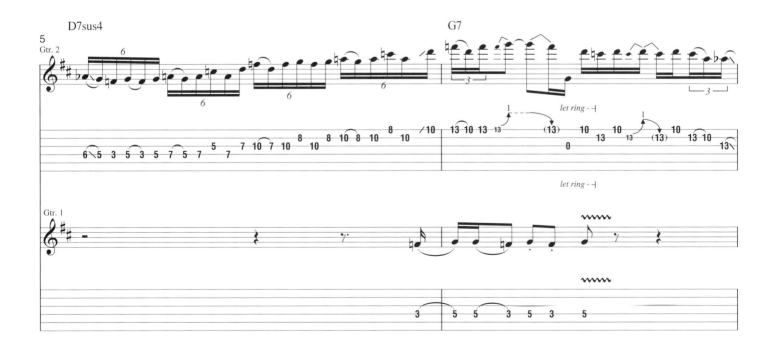

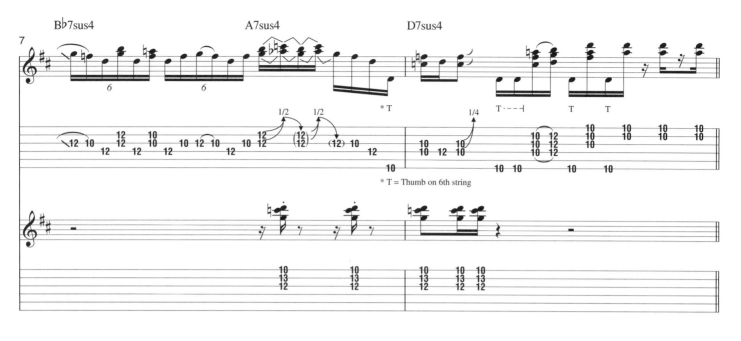

* T = Thumb on 6th string

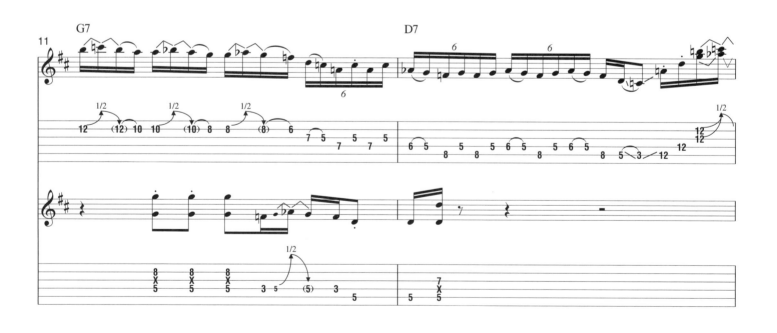

Figure 13—Section G **(Guitar Solo 2)**

The second proper solo break occurs at approximately 3:02 on the original recording. Tommy's soloing over the bridge changes here and opens with some sparse statements from D minor pentatonic in measures 1 and 2. This quickly gives way to a smooth, legato sextuplet ascent in measure 3, culminating in a pedal-steel bend emulation at the beginning of measure 4. Don't miss the 1 1/2-step pre-bend and release in measure 4 that sounds amazingly slide guitar-like.

Over the E7 in measure 7, T.E. rips off a doozy of a run that's very reminiscent of the late "Master of the Telecaster," Danny Gatton (though the title is shared by the late Albert Collins as well). Beginning with a set of high-range double stops segueing into open-position composite blues scale riffery, the snaky phrase gives way to an ultra-cool natural harmonic at fret 5 on string 3, which is treated to a whole-step bend and vibrato executed *behind the nut*, Jerry Donahue-style.

Performance Tip: A Tele- or Strat-style guitar without a locking nut will be necessary to pull off the behind-the-nut bend in measure 8. The effect *could* be simulated with a whammy bar that's set up to allow the pitch to be raised (Floyd Rose), but it just wouldn't look as cool!

Fig. 13

FROM THE HIP
(*Determination*, 1992)

By Tommy Emmanuel

To many new fans, the music that fills Emmanuel's earlier albums like *Up from Down Under* (1987), *Dare to Be Different* (1990), and *Determination* (1992) sound worlds apart from the acoustic fingerstyle mastery they've come to expect from him as of late. But a closer listen to these albums reveals that he's always had a soft spot for acoustic guitar, and it is featured quite prominently. Nevertheless, there is plenty of burning electric guitar work that should not be forgotten. "From the Hip" is a prime example.

Figure 14—Sections A (Intro) and B (Theme)

"From the Hip" is a bright, uptempo rocker clocking in at 240 bpm. Needless to say, it's not for the faint of heart. With ensemble hits, syncopated stops, and octave-spanning melodies, there's never a dull moment. The song kicks off with Emmanuel palm-muting a low tonic G note in steady eighth notes to get the momentum going. Aside from the low F notes used to bookend each two-measure phrase, he also throws in a mean little blues lick (measure 11) to pass the time. In measure 14, things are ready to really get underway, and the band kick-starts the song's vitals with a set of B♭5–F5 ensemble hits that's repeated four times.

As if shooting "from the hip," Emmanuel's entrance with the main theme at the pickup to measure 18 takes the listener a bit off guard. This is partly due to the syncopated rhythm but also because it begins on the 4th (C). He doesn't hang out there long, though, and before you can even reach for your holster, he's already winded his way down over the tonic G5 chord through almost two octaves, mixing major and minor blues sounds along the way. The sassy B♭ that ends the first antecedent phrase in measure 21 is replaced by the tough-sounding F note in measure 25 for the consequent phrase. For the C5 chord (IV) in measures 26–29, he begins similarly, recasting the notes to fit the new harmony, but soon embarks on a triad workout, speeding through C, B♭, and Am forms before coming to rest on a Gm form to imply a C9 sound in measures 28–29.

After another statement of the original melody over G5 in measures 30–33, he begins to navigate the non-standard changes of B♭–A♭ in measures 34–35. Beginning with a G Dorian (G–A–B♭–C–D–E–F) line over B♭, he switches to G blues for the A♭ chord, hammering out an A♭ triad on beat 1 of measure 36 and snaking his way down to a G triad by way of a demented-sounding series of chromatically descending seventh chord fragments before closing the section off with the ensemble B♭5–F5 hits.

Fig. 14

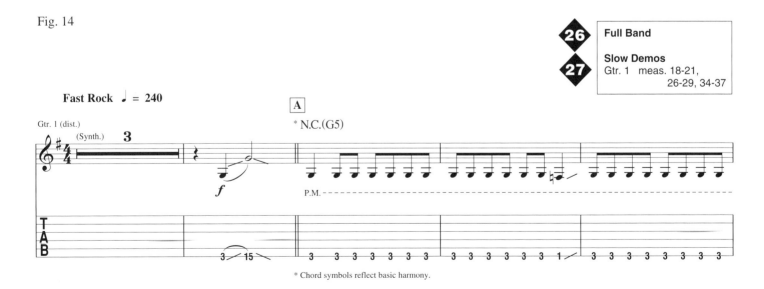

* Chord symbols reflect basic harmony.

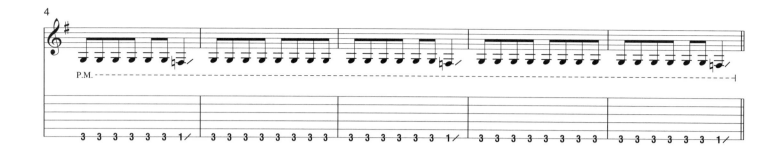

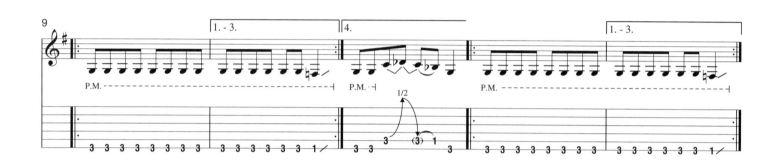

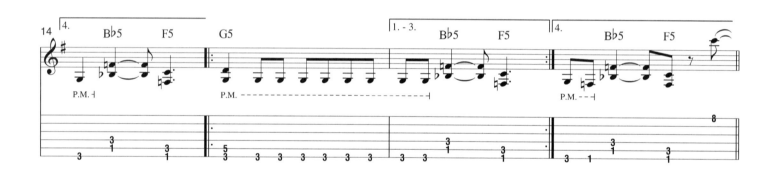

Figure 15—Section C **(Bridge)**

For the bridge (section C), Emmanuel contrasts things in a big way. Opening things wide up, the band downshifts into a half-time feel while Emmanuel floats over the ethereal changes of measures 1–12 with a mournful, aching melody. The tonality is skewed a bit here, as the progression seems to have one foot in G minor and one in G major. At measure 13, the band leaps to its feet again, grinding out a Latin-style beat while Emmanuel transposes the same syncopated melody down three times in whole steps to match the transposing progression of Am–F, Gm–E♭, and Fm–D♭ before resolving to a high D note. It's at this point that we realize we're heading back to the key of G, and this D is acting as the V chord. And, as Emmanuel is prone to do, he delays this resolution for several measures, filling the space with another winding triadic line moving down via whole steps (D–C–B♭–A♭), before settling into the home base of G5 on beat 4 of measure 23. Emmanuel's not quite ready to wrap it up yet, so he crams in one more octave-spanning G blues run in measures 25–26.

Performance Tip: At this tempo, the triad work is not easy by any means. Try working with different pick strokes to see what feels most natural for you. Perhaps hybrid picking would work well, too.

Fig. 15

38

Figure 16—Section D **(Guitar Solo 1)**

For the solo (section D), the key moves up a half step to A♭, and Emmanuel hits the ground running with a demented little rhythmic motive that he melodically mutates twice over before coming back home to resolve on the tonic A♭ in measure 3. Things begin harmlessly enough in measure 1 with a line from the A♭ major scale, but by measure 2, it's only recognizable by the rhythmic imitation—this seems more like a fun fingering pattern than any particular scalar concept. By measure 4, though, he's off and running in A♭ blues territory, bending his way through pentatonic licks and blurring Dorian-based double stops. Over the D♭ (IV) chord in measures 9–12, he snakes his way through a jazzy line that would be just as home in a Bird (Charlie Parker) solo. Fundamentally, he's working out of A♭ Dorian here (A♭–B♭–C♭–D♭–E♭–F–G♭), or D♭ *Mixolydian* if you prefer, but the included chromatic tones and the articulations are really what lends the jazz sound to the phrase.

Emmanuel leaps dramatically to the higher register over the tonic A♭ chord in measure 13 with a series of half-step bends from C to D♭ and follows up with more gutsy double stops in measure 15 before going A♭ major pentatonic in the "B.B. box" over the E♭ (V) chord in measures 17–18. After a soaring bend of G♭ to A♭ in measures 19–20, Emmanuel closes it out in style with a "countrified" double-stop/pull-off lick that would make Pete Anderson proud.

Fig. 16

30 Full Band

31 Slow Demos
Gtr. 1 meas. 1-24

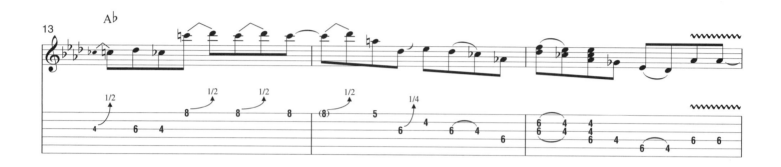

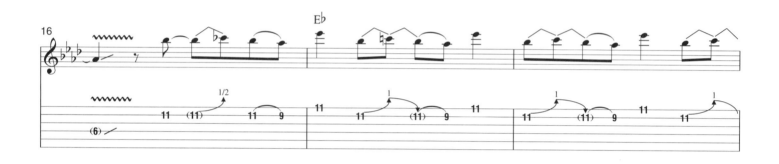

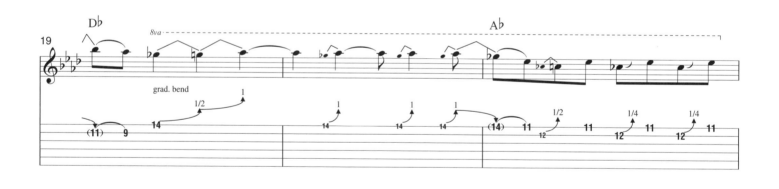

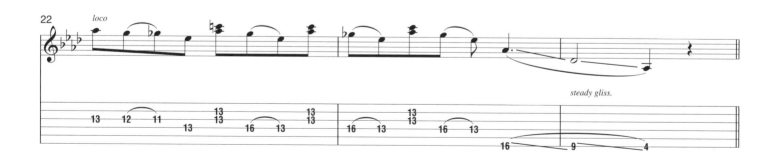

GUITAR BOOGIE SHUFFLE
(*Dare to Be Different*, 1990)
By Arthur Smith

Tommy Emmanuel originally recorded his version of Arthur Smith's "Guitar Boogie Shuffle" (retitled as simply "Guitar Boogie") as an electric piece on *Dare to Be Different*. Though Emmanuel has long been a guitar legend in his native Australia and to those guitarists and musicians "in the know," he's finally begun to enjoy the worldwide recognition and success he deserves. One of the reasons? Youtube. Search "Tommy Emmanuel" on the site, and you'll see one acoustic version in particular of "Guitar Boogie Shuffle" with nearly five million views and thousands of comments all saying basically the same thing: "Holy sh*t!" In fact, the song has been affectionately renamed "the YouTube song" as a result.

Figure 17—Section A (Theme)

This high-octane rockabilly number is based on a 12-bar blues in E and begins, as many guitar shuffles do, with a low-register boogie pattern played in mostly constant eighth notes. Two things are key here: groove and conviction. Emmanuel has both in spades. In true rockabilly fashion, he has a slapback echo applied to his clean guitar, which is also doubled on the recording.

To keep things interesting, Emmanuel dresses up the basic boogie figure with grace-note slides throughout, hammer-on/pull-off triplets (measures 2, 4, 10), and bending riffs (measure 6). The latter is particularly striking, as the sustained note breaks up the monotony of the constant eighth-note onslaught. For the turnaround in measures 11–12, Emmanuel goes out in style, splitting the two guitars into separate parts. Gtr. 1 rips a nasty blues run in open position, mixing major and minor 3rds and jabbing at the blue note (Bb) twice before landing with force on the open low E for the start of the next chorus. Gtr. 2 plays it old-school-style with classic, chromatically descending double stops against the open high E string.

Performance Tip: Alternate picking is absolutely essential during the boogie patterns of measures 1–10 for proper groove. Make sure you're pairing downbeats with down-strokes, and really dig in.

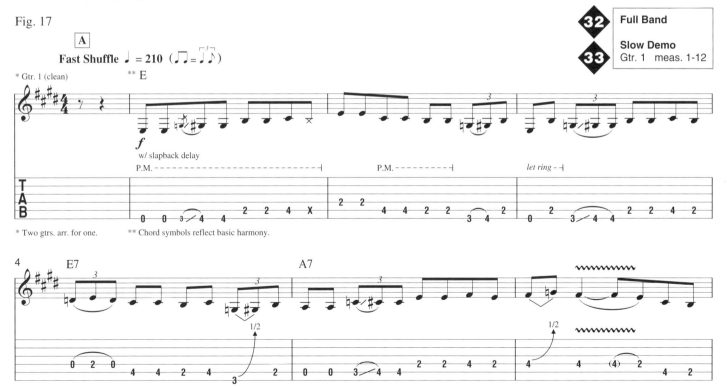

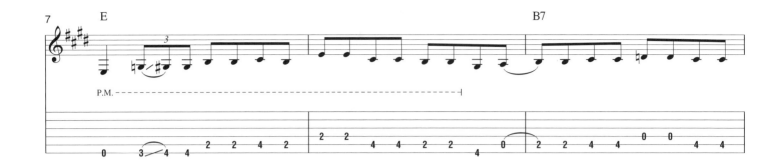

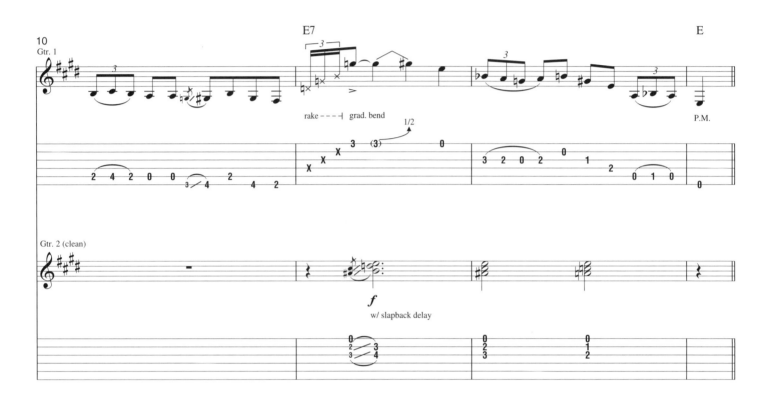

Figure 18—Section <u>C</u> **(Guitar Solo)**

For the first proper guitar solo of the piece, Tommy Emmanuel jumps up to twelfth position, opening with a classic pickup phrase consisting of the minor 3rd (G) hammered to the major 3rd (G♯) followed by the 5th (B) and 6th (C♯). He then pecks out several staccato tonic E notes in measure 1 to get things underway. By measure 2, he's already twisting fingers every which way with winding composite blues phrases, reaching down to a low B note on string 5 before climbing all the way back up to squawk out some half-step bends from the 2nd (F♯) to the tart ♭3rd (G).

He rips through the IV chord in measures 5–6 with a repeated triplet figure, C–C♯–E, which transposes the blues-approved minor-to-major 3rd approach for the A7 harmony. Over the I chord in measures 7–8, he treads water mostly in preparation for what's coming next. In measures 9–10, Emmanuel mows over the V chord (B7) with a chromatic-laced sixteenth-note line, arranged four notes per string, that sounds like Danny Cedrone's famous "Rock Around the Clock" solo on steroids. By the way, measures 1–8 of Emmanuel's solo are very similar to Arthur Smith's original from his 1948 recording—obviously a nod to the influential late great picker. If you haven't yet heard Smith's recording, it's more than worth checking out. 1940's or not, there's some great guitar playing on that record.

Fig. 18

Figure 19—Sections E (Guitar Solo 2) and F (Harmonized Solo)

Emmanuel begins his second solo with a classic blues technique: the moaning, gradually released bend. Over the span of two measures, he milks a whole-step bend from the 4th (A) to the 5th (B) for all it's worth, slowly releasing it as he picks the string in steady eighth notes. As with chromatic, "outside" excursions, the effectiveness of a trick like this depends heavily on its resolution, and Emmanuel falls right into a tough, minor pentatonic phrase to cap it off nicely.

In measure 9, he tap dances around the V chord (B7) by jabbing at a B6 voicing and moving it chromatically down and up with syncopated rhythm. Emmanuel caps off the chorus in measures 11–12 with a nod to his idol, Chet, burning through an open-position rockabilly lick that uses a symmetrical fingering pattern on strings 1–3. Though this lick is all about the flash, for the curious, the notes involved form an E Dorian/blues hybrid scale (E–F♯–G–A–B♭–B–C♯–D).

For the second chorus, beginning in measure 13, Emmanuel joins himself via overdub for a harmonized melody laced with chromatics and arpeggios throughout. The harmony is exclusively in 3rds, save for the occasional 4th during an arpeggiated line (measures 17 and 20). For the B7 chord in measures 21–22, Emmanuel splits a triad line between the two parts, with one guitar playing dyads on strings 1 and 2 and the other playing dyads on strings 2 and 3, resulting in a doubled unison note on string 2.

Performance Tip: If you're the only guitarist, it is actually possible to arrange the harmonized section for one guitar. Though it wouldn't be easy, it would be quite rewarding—not to mention quite impressive to an audience!

Fig. 19

36 Full Band

37 Slow Demos
Gtr. 1   meas. 11-12

Figure 20—Section H (Outro-Guitar Solo)

In section H, Emmanuel seizes one more opportunity to shred. While Gtr. 3 provides horn-like, syncopated chord stabs, Tommy (as Gtr. 1) tears it up mostly in the open position with Stevie Ray-type composite blues scale runs. In fact, these lines would be very reminiscent of Stevie if it weren't for the trebly Tele tone used. In measures 3–4, Emmanuel lets loose with a trademark major pentatonic sequence in triplets—no small feat considering the tempo of 210 bpm. After tremolo-picking an E/G double stop through the A7 (functioning as its 5th/♭7th), he erupts into a repeated, descending blues scale lick in open position that flows through the I chord in measures 7–8 and the V chord in measure 9. Note how the pull-offs used here not only facilitate the speed but also contribute to the slippery, legato sound.

In measure 10, over the A chord, he disengages from the repetition smoothly by expanding on the previous blues run, even anticipating the coming I chord of measure 11 by hammering on to the G♯ in beat 3. He doesn't rest for long after resolving to the tonic E note in measure 11 via the classic G–G♯ slide, continuing up the E major pentatonic scale and climaxing in fifth position with a pedal steel-sounding bend from the 2nd (F♯) to the major 3rd (G♯).

Performance Tip: For the repeated blues scale lick in measures 7–9, plant yourself in second position. This will allow you to access the B♭ and A notes on string 3 with fingers 2 and 1, respectively, and the E note on string 4 with finger 1.

Fig. 20

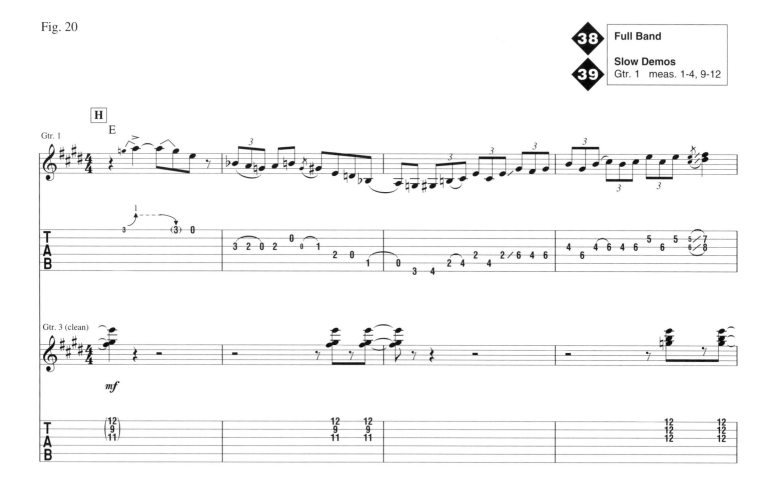

THE HUNT
(*Classical Gas*, 1996)

By Tommy Emmanuel

For the *Classical Gas* album (1996), Tommy Emmanuel was backed by the Australian Philharmonic Orchestra. This luxury was certainly not wasted, as Emmanuel's compositions are expansive and worthy of such a grandiose production. Aside from the popular title track, "The Hunt" is a veritable guitar suite, complete with virtuosic displays and epic themes.

Figure 21—Sections A (Intro) and B (Theme 1)

For "The Hunt," T.E. tunes to Drop D tuning, which only requires the low E string to be tuned down one whole step. This provides octave D notes on strings 6 and 4, of which Emmanuel makes good use. The introduction sets the stage with a high-energy, chugging strum riff somewhat similar to Zeppelin's "Song Remains the Same." In measures 1–2, over the continuous D-string drone, Emmanuel pits triads D, Dsus2, F, and G on top, establishing a classic rock-sounding vocabulary. For measures 3–4, he rides along Dsus2 until beats 3 and 4 of the latter, at which point he bookends the phrase with sharp Csus2 and G/B chords. This entire four-measure phrase (Rhy. Fig. 1) is repeated to round out the intro.

Once things are underway, Emmanuel wastes no time dropping jaws in section B. Using the open D chord as a harmonic backdrop, he answers each measure's opening strum with a sixteenth-note run from the D major scale in open position. Hammer-ons and pull-offs are used throughout these runs, resulting in a smooth, blurred articulation. In measure 12, he caps off a four-measure phrase with Csus2–G/B, just as in the intro. After repeating this first four-measure phrase (measures 13–16), Tommy really puts the pedal to the medal. Expanding upon the single-note theme, he answers introductory D chord strums with a D major scale run covering nearly two octaves that may even send Yngwie to the shed for a good while. Each run concludes with chord punches that include a measure of 2/4, resulting in a slightly lopsided feel to the phrasing. After three times, the new expanded theme is capped off in measures 26–27 with a strummed progression of B♭sus2–F6/9(no 3rd), or ♭VI–♭III in the key of D.

Performance Tip: Developing the relaxation necessary to quickly switch from the robust strumming to the intricate single-note picking required here is no small feat and will only come with lots *and lots* of practice.

Fig. 21

Gtr. 1: Drop D tuning:
(low to high) D–A–D–G–B–E

40 Full Band

41 Slow Demo
Gtr. 1 meas. 1-4,
9-10, 17-22

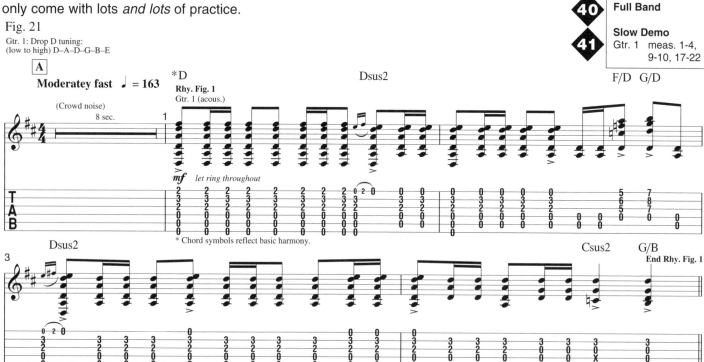

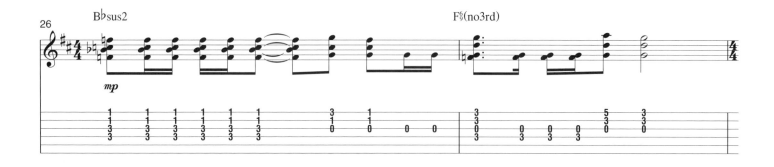

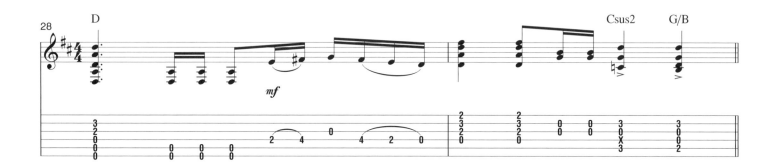

Figure 22—Section C (Theme 2)

After the frantic onslaught of notes in section B, relief is provided in section C with a lyrical, half-time feel theme played on distorted electric guitar (Gtr. 2) supported by arpeggios played by Gtr. 1. The tonality is a bit skewed at this point, as the C–G/B–B♭6–F/A progression in measures 1–4 seems to have more in common with the *parallel* key of D minor. When the four-measure phrase repeats in measures 5–8, our suspicion is confirmed, as the A7 chord (substituted for the F/A of measure 4) in measure 8 supports a D harmonic minor melody and does indeed resolve to a Dm chord in measure 9.

This new established D minor tonality in measure 9 also marks a change in texture, as Gtr. 1 begins strumming through full chords in accompaniment. Things are still not entirely tidy, though, as a G/D (found in the parallel D *major* mode) chord in measures 10 and 14 clouds the tonality yet again. The final V chord (A) of the section in measure 16 is extended (one of Emmanuel's favorite devices) with alternating B♭/A and A chords, while Gtr. 2 soars atop with a high A note bent up a half step to B♭ before settling into a long, sustained, vibratoed A note.

In measure 20, we finally arrive into full-fledged D minor territory with a syncopated ensemble chord figure: Dm–C–Dm–C–B♭–A. This two-measure progression is heard three times before a four-measure answering progression of Gm–Gm6–Asus4–A brings us back to the main theme (not shown). Gtr. 1 heightens this dramatic return with tremolo-picked dyads on strings 1 and 2, while Gtr. 2 sustains G5 and A5 power chords.

Fig. 22

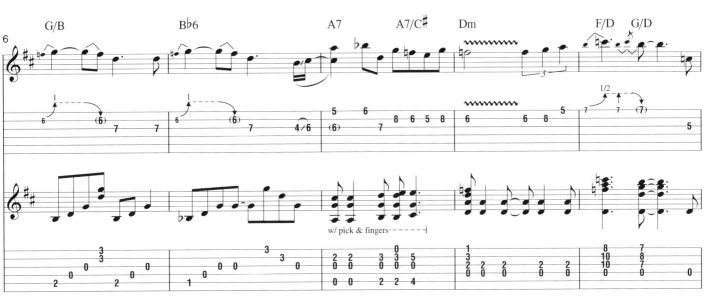

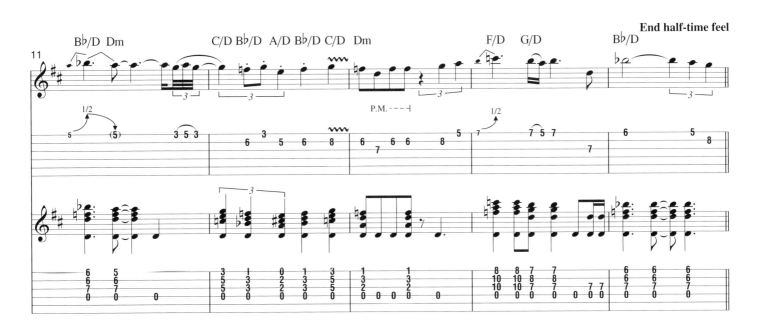

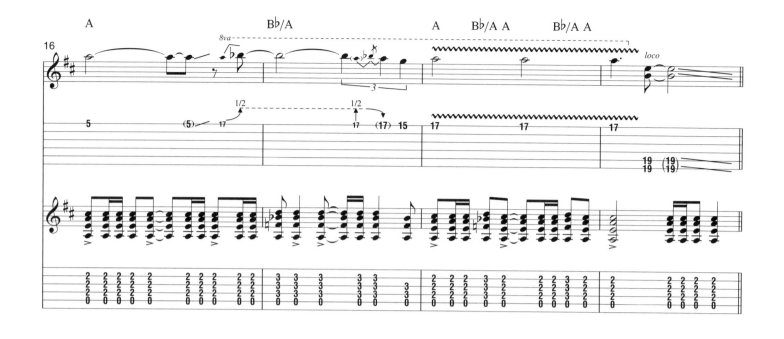

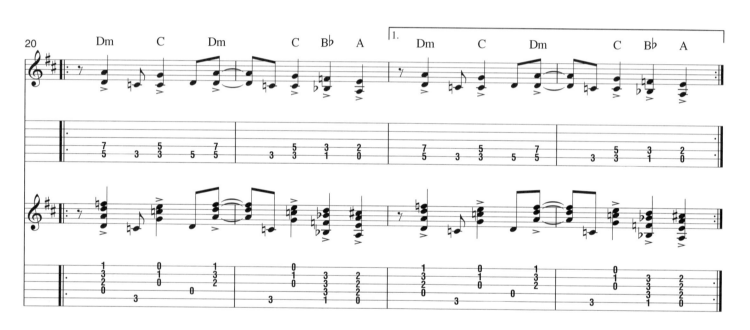

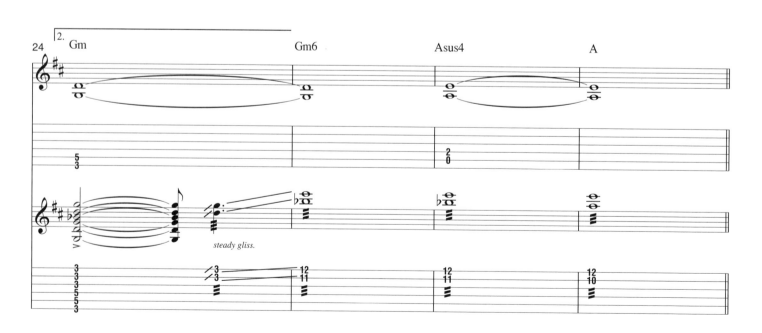

INITIATION
(*Up from Down Under*, 1987)
By Tommy Emmanuel

"Initiation," as Tommy explains in several live versions, tells the story of an Aboriginal (indigenous Australian) ceremony and a boy's journey to manhood. Though Emmanuel usually starts the song nowadays with spooky sound effects generated by knocks and scratches on his acoustic guitar (made more striking with use of the delay pedal), the song first appeared in a more straightforward version on 1987's *Up from Down Under*. With nary a flashy measure to be seen, T.E. demonstrates his softer, pensive side on this track.

Figure 23—Sections A (Intro) and B (Theme 1)

After a brief percussion intro (not shown), Emmanuel begins the ceremony with a lone, low E string in eighth notes. What the listener doesn't know at first is that this droning, low E note will continue through practically the entire piece. Throughout the 11-measure intro, Emmanuel splashes bits of E minor tonality atop the E string via harmonics (measure 3), dyads and single notes (measures 5–7), and triads (measures 7–9). A delay set for quarter-note regeneration with two repeats adds depth to the harmonic punctuations throughout. All the notes are contained within the E natural minor scale (E–F♯–G–A–B–C–D) until measure 8, where Emmanuel draws from E *melodic minor* (E–F♯–G–A–B–C♯–D♯) with A and B7 triads, resolving to Em once again at the end of measure 9 to effectively bring the intro to a close.

In section B, he locks into a rhythmic chordal figure atop the droning E bass, changing chords on the last eighth note of each measure. Em and D/E harmonies alternate until measure 18, when a B7/E chord closes off an eight-measure phrase. This eight-measure phrase is repeated with minor variations in measures 20–27, but Emmanuel tacks on one more B7–Em change in measures 28–29 to bookend the section. Take note of the various hammer-ons and slides used throughout that help decorate the harmonies.

Performance Tip: This piece will require a strong sense of right-hand independence. Your thumb needs to hold down constant eighth notes while your fingers pluck all sorts of different rhythms. Practice chugging along on the low E string, adding bits on top slowly but surely, until you don't even need to think about the bass.

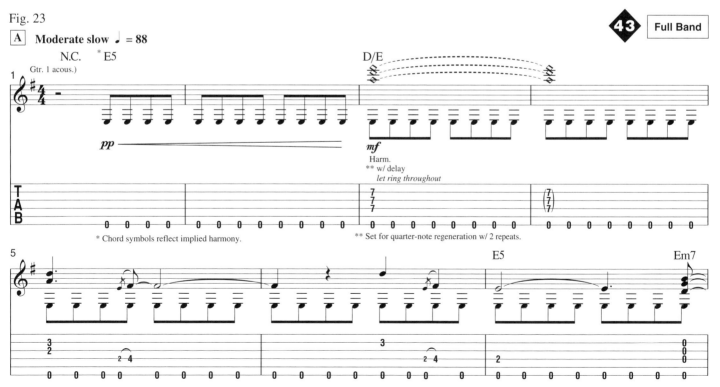

Fig. 23

Figure 24—Section C (Theme 2)

Section C begins with a move to the iv chord, Am, which is broken across two beats. This M.O. continues in measure 2 with a broken Bm triad spanning 1 1/2 beats and a C triad on the "and" of beat 2. Your right-hand independence will be tested even more so in the abbreviated 2/4 measure 3, where you're required to pick a sixteenth-note melody (though brief) against the eighth-note bass line. In measures 6–7, Emmanuel drifts steadily upward in range, nabbing several different B7 inversions and variations along the way, coming to rest in measure 7 with D#/F#/C. Taken altogether, this implies a B7♭9 sound over E—a tense sonority indeed. The tension subsides in measure 8 with an Em9 cluster voicing that requires a good stretch. He arpeggiates through this form in measures 9 and adds a low D note to create an Em9 tonality before closing the section once again with a V–i move in measures 10–11.

Fig. 24

Figure 25—Section E (Bridge)

In section E, we hear the most colorful harmonies of the entire piece, and Emmanuel begins right off the bat with an E° chord. While this is certainly ear-grabbing, it's not nearly as much as the Eadd9–F#m11/E–Eadd9 move that follows in measures 3–4, which comes straight out of the parallel E major mode. Order is quickly restored in measures 7–8 with a iv–V–i move (Am–B7/E–Em) to once establish the E minor tonality. Emmanuel is not yet finished with his antics, though, and in measures 11–14, he turns out an Em6–F/E–Em9–B7/E progression in austere fashion, plucking each chord on the downbeat and sustaining it throughout the measure before reconnecting with the main theme (not shown). As demonstrated in this section and throughout the entire piece, Emmanuel is a master of chord inversions and makes use of various forms on all areas of the neck.

Fig. 25

LEWIS & CLARK
(*The Mystery*, 2006)

By Tommy Emmanuel

The Mystery was released in 2006 and is focused almost squarely on the acoustic guitar, as has been Tommy's focus for years now. In fact, many new fans are quite surprised to learn how thoroughly Emmanuel had mastered the electric before moving on to concentrate so heavily on acoustic and, specifically, the fingerstyle genre. Emmanuel composed "Lewis & Clark" after reading through the famed explorers' journals. It's a unique, somewhat haunting solo piece that's executed with effortless grace—par for the course with T.E.

Figure 26—Section A **(Intro)**

Note: Emmanuel is fingering in the key of Em, but the capo on the second fret causes the song to sound in the key of F♯m. For simplicity, the following analysis will be in Em, and all pitch references will be in relation to the guitar key—not sounding pitch.

Emmanuel begins "Lewis & Clark" with a free-time intro, dividing the guitar into basically melody on top and bass note on bottom. The bass notes are sparse, leaving plenty of room for the light, whistling melody. Derived mostly from the E minor *hexatonic scale* (E–F♯–G–A–B–D) with the occasional B♭ borrowed from the E blues scale for ornaments, it's got a distinct Native American flavor and paints a picture of an untouched, primitive landscape with an eagle sailing majestically above.

He loosely outlines a i (Em)–♭VI (C)–♭VII (D)–IV (A5) progression, where each chord lasts for two measures, to create an eight-measure phrase. Over the A5, he deliberately avoids the 3rd (C or C♯), instead rolling through an A5 arpeggio that includes a unison E note via the open first string. This creates a bit of ambiguity, as it's almost as if he wants to venture into E Dorian territory by including the major 6th (C♯). Emmanuel repeats this same progression again, however, and over the IV chord in measure 16, he does commit to a C♯, which indicates a temporary shift to an E Dorian (E–F♯–G–A–B–C♯–D) tonality. He closes out the intro with a slow, arpeggiated climb up the tonic Em chord, mixing open strings, fretted notes, and natural harmonics.

Performance Tip: Take note of the *let ring* indication in the music. In measure 1, Emmanuel holds down the E note on string 2 with the third finger while using the fourth finger to slide from A to B♭ and back to pull off on string 1. This isn't easy to do, but it is possible with a bit of practice.

Fig. 26
Gtr. 1: Capo II

* Symbols in parentheses represent chords respective to capoed guitar. Symbols above reflect actual sounding chords. Capoed fret is "0" in tab. Chord symbols reflect implied harmony.

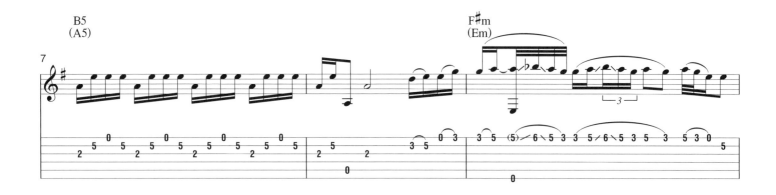

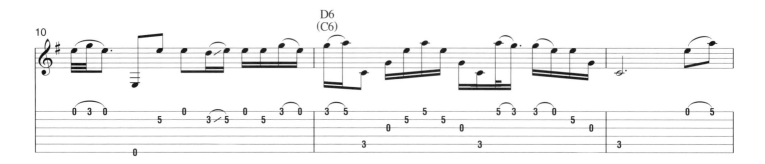

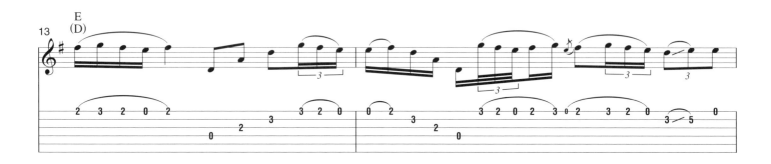

Figure 27—Section B (Theme 1)

For section B, Emmanuel embarks on a Travis picking-based journey through modal mixture and beautiful melody. He begins in measures 1–12, volleying back and forth between Em and G chords. Notice the open-string hammer-on technique that Emmanuel uses to kick off each measure of Em, providing an extra bit of rhythmic propulsion to his already substantial groove. He decorates the proceedings in measure 8 over the G chord with a completely independent D–C#–B–A melody, once again confirming the E Dorian tonality—for now, anyway!

Measure 12 can be thought of as a pickup to the actual theme that starts in measure 13. At this point, the modal mixing begins, as Emmanuel harmonizes a lovely melody on the treble strings with a Travis-picked ♭VII (D)–IV (A)–I (E)–♭III (G) four-measure progression. This phrase is repeated with slight variation (on the IV chord) in measures 17–20 and begins to repeat a third time in measure 21. After the first D and A chords, though, Emmanuel remains on the E for two measures and closes out the phrase with a measure of ♭VI (C) and ♭VII (D) before returning to the Em–G groove.

Like the master Chet himself, Emmanuel's separation between melody and accompaniment here is nothing short of amazing. His melodies speak with such clarity that you'd swear he was playing nothing else, much less maintaining a rock-steady Travis picking pattern at the same time. This comes with serious practice and experience; you need to reach the point where you don't even need to think about the thumb anymore.

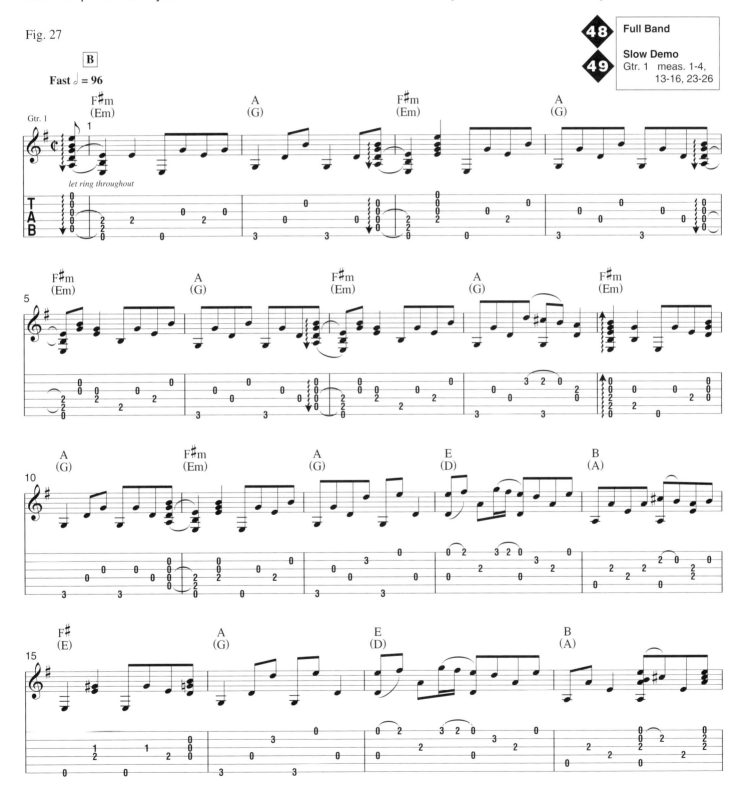

Fig. 27

Figure 28—Section C (Theme 2)

To contrast the flowing main theme, Emmanuel pecks out a more choked-sounding theme in section C. He lowers his dynamic level and slightly mutes the bass notes with his palm, while allowing the top strings to ring. If the i (Em11)–♭VI (C6/9)–♭VII (D)–IV (Asus2) progression sounds familiar, it's because the same one was used to open the piece for the introduction, where it sounded in free time.

On top, Emmanuel works mostly with dyads on strings 1 and 2. Note that the same melody in measures 1–2 over Em is reharmonized in measures 3–4 with a C6/9 voicing. The melody used over the D and Asus2 chords in measures 5–6 and 7–8, respectively, is an interesting augmentation of the one used for the same chords in section B, where the chords change every measure. Another change in texture for this section occurs in the bass. Emmanuel has discontinued playing the bass on every beat and instead, on the Em and C6/9 chords, is playing mostly half notes. Further investigation reveals that, in measures 2 and 4 (as well as measure 10 during the repeat of the progression), he syncopates the second bass note so that it appears on the "and" of beat 2 instead of squarely on it. Even further study indicates the reasoning for this: the melody is syncopated in measures 1 and 3, but it's not in measures 2 and 4. So the melody and bass are playing around each other to help fill up the spaces. This is good evidence of the thought that Emmanuel puts into his arrangements; he's not just on autopilot once he settles into a pattern.

For the repeat of this phrase, Emmanuel extends the D chord to four measures, thinning out to a single melody in measure 16. He then extends the following Asus2 chord to four measures and again bookends those measures with a single melody derived from the E Dorian mode before settling back into the Em–G groove from the main theme.

Performance Tip: For the Em11 and C6/9 chords, Emmanuel flattens his second finger to barre strings 1 and 2, which can be kind of tricky if you're not used to doing this. One alternative is to use a 1–2–3 fingering (low to high) for the C6/9 chord, hammering to the A note on string 1 with the pinky. For the D chords in measures 14-15, he strums down-and-up on beats 2 and 4 with his index and middle fingers, Paul McCartney-style.

Fig. 28

SINCE WE MET

(*Only*, 2002)

Words and Music by Tommy Emmanuel

Only is Tommy's first, fully solo acoustic album and was released in the States on Steve Vai's Favored Nations label. Filled to the brim with fingerstyle mastery, it's a treasure for long-time admirers of Emmanuel's acoustic playing.

Figure 29—Sections A **(Intro) and** B **(Theme 1)**

Note: Emmanuel is fingering in the key of A, but the capo on the second fret causes the song to sound in the key of B. For simplicity, the following analysis will be in A, and all pitch references will be in relation to the guitar key—not sounding pitch.

"Since We Met" is in the key of A major and is slightly reminiscent of Eric Clapton's "Tears in Heaven" with regards to the tempo and main chord progression. Emmanuel begins with a four-measure intro (section A) that sets up the key by running through a I (A)–V (E/G♯)–♭VII (G6)–IV (Dadd9/F♯) progression in measures 1–3 before capping off the section with I–V in measure 4. Mixing arpeggios with plucked chords and bass notes, the emphasis here is on creating a full-range sound—not necessarily singling out any one element (melody, chords, or bass). In measure 3, he rolls up and back down through the Dadd9/F♯ for dramatic effect, and at the end of measure 4, he kicks off the beginning of the main theme in style with a legato, bass-line run of E–F♯–G♯–A.

For the main theme B , Emmanuel separates the melody from the accompaniment and bass with characteristic ease. The original four-measure phrase of I (A)–IV (E/G♯)–vi (F♯m)–iii (C♯m)–IV (D)–ii (Bm7) V (E) is repeated in the next four measures with only a minor variation: the final measure (12) contains only the V chord instead of ii–V. In measure 13, Emmanuel begins wandering into modal mixture territory, moving through ♭VII (G), IV (D), ♭VI (Fadd9), and ♭III (C), before restoring order with a ii–V in measure 17, which leads back to the main theme again (not shown). Note that the use of inversions (D/F♯ and C/E) creates the chromatically descending bass line G–F♯–F–E in measures 13–16.

Performance Tip: Regarding the right hand, there isn't really any set pattern at work here, so you can experiment and see what works best. The tempo is slow enough that it's not terribly critical to work out specifics.

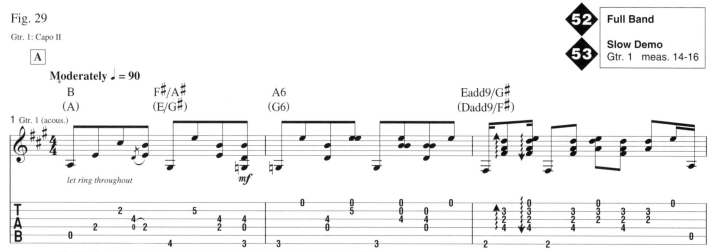

Fig. 29

Gtr. 1: Capo II

52 Full Band

53 Slow Demo
Gtr. 1 meas. 14-16

* Symbols in parentheses represent chods respective to capoed guitar. Symbols above reflect actual sounding chords. Capoed fret is "0" in tab. Chord symbols reflect implied harmony.

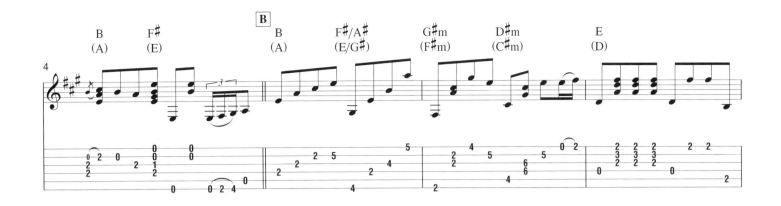

Figure 30—Section C **(Theme 2)**

The texture remains relatively the same for section C , but Emmanuel uses another device to provide contrast: *range*. Both melody and bass notes start off an octave higher here. Interestingly, though the melody is different from the start, the chord progression begins in a manner similar to section B with A–E/G♯–F♯m–Esus4 changes in measures 1–2 before veering into new territory with D and C in measures 3 and 4, respectively. Emmanuel makes use of 6ths on top of the tonic A chord, giving way to single notes and broken triads in measures 2–4. Also of note are the strategically placed percussive ticks, which are created by forcefully planting the right hand on the strings. Be aware that these all occur on either beat 2 or 4—i.e., the "backbeat"—which somewhat simulates a light snare drum played with brushes.

After beginning to repeat the first four-measure phrase in measure 5, Emmanuel quickly changes course with iii–vi (measure 7), ii–♭III (measure 8), ♭VI (Fmaj7/A, measure 9), and V (E/G♯, measure 10). Repeating the ♭VI–V move makes for a 12-measure section. Note the bluesy ornament of A–B–C–B in measure 12 articulated with a combination of hammer-ons and slides. On clear display here, as with the rest of this piece, is evidence of Emmanuel's willingness to veer from conventional fingerstyle patterns if it best suits the piece. Just because you can, you don't *always* have to hit a bass note on the downbeat of each measure, and you don't *always* have to have three parts (melody, chords, and bass) present. Sometimes, just using those elements in tandem works perfectly.

Fig. 30

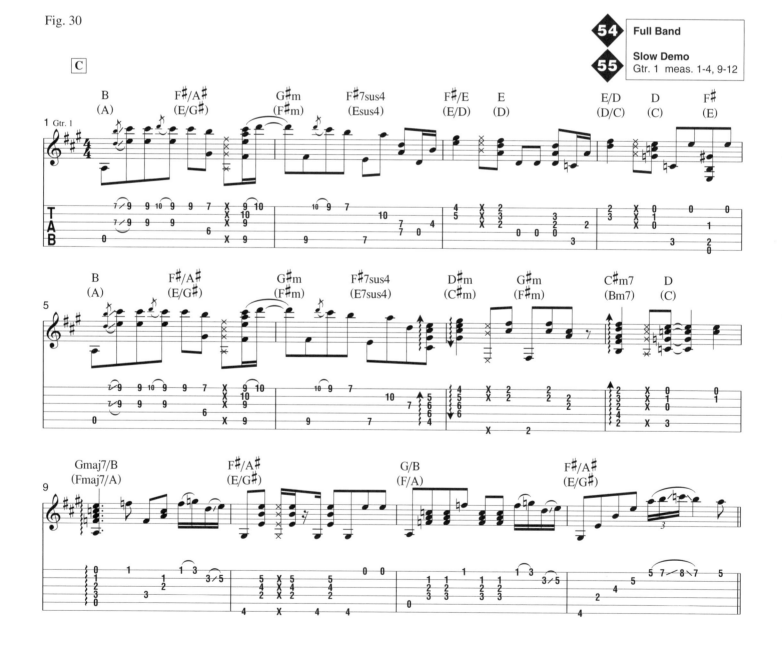

54 Full Band

55 Slow Demo
Gtr. 1 meas. 1-4, 9-12

UP FROM DOWN UNDER
(*Up from Down Under*, 1987)
By Tommy Emmanuel and Alan Mansfield

The second song that we'll examine in this volume from the *Up from Down Under* album is the title track. With a light, funk beat and a style that can safely be categorized as smooth jazz, the song sounds, not surprisingly, quite similar to what Chet Atkins was doing in the mid-to-late eighties. Though the acoustic is featured, Emmanuel does lay down some clean-tone electric complete with a chorus effect. Hey, it was the eighties!

Figure 31—Section A (Intro)

Emmanuel opens "Up from Down Under" with a masterpiece of solo acoustic guitar, and his Chet influence is on full display here. Previewing the basic chord structure of the main theme to come, he works in free time, playing mostly arpeggios and plucking out melody notes on top. The song is in the key of G and is filled with jazzy changes that sound somewhat reminiscent of a Christmas standard. In measure 4, he creates a pretty Em11 voicing using natural harmonics at fret 12. For the Am11 in measures 7–9, he glides effortlessly through a stream of *harp harmonics*—Lenny Breau/Chet Atkins-style. This technique blends normally-plucked notes with artificial harmonics to create a harp-like sound. Along with Eric Johnson, T.E. carries the torch as another current true master of this technique.

Take note of the A9 voicing in measure 13, which mixes open strings 1 (E) and 2 (B) with fretted notes on strings 3 (C♯) and 4 (G). This is another favorite Chet device that Emmanuel's added to his bag of tricks. After an extended stay on the V chord (D11–D°7–D7) in measures 15–16, he arppegiates a colorful F13 (♭VII) chord in measure 17 and another fretted/open-string combination Am9 voicing in measure 18. To close out the intro, he pulls off an even more dazzling display of harp harmonics than earlier, this time mixing in hammer-ons and pull-offs to create diatonic seven-note scales as opposed to the pentatonic scales achieved with the often-used one-finger barre form.

Performance Tip: For the harp harmonics (H.H.), use the third finger of the right hand to pluck the normal notes. To create the harmonic, touch the harmonic point with your R.H. first finger and pluck the string with your thumb. Your right hand will be hovering over the fretboard the entire time—in this case, around the seventeenth fret.

Fig. 31

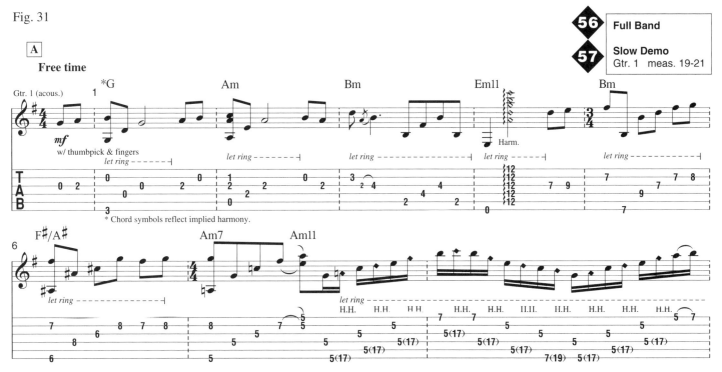

Figure 32—Section B (Theme)

The band enters for the main theme, and Tommy floats above the electric keys, fretless bass, and reverb-drenched drums with a clear, round acoustic tone. He's moved exclusively to a single-note melody here, and closer examination reveals that his unaccompanied intro forecast much of the melodic material presented here. After a four-measure phrase comprising of I–vi–ii–V and iii–V/iii–ii–V (two chords per measure), Gtr. 2 (elec.) joins in support of a repeat of the phrase, ringing arpeggios and adding the occasional, eighties-approved, single-note palm-muted riff (measure 8). Aside from a bluesy, half-step bend of E to F♮ over the Am11 chords in measures 4 and 8, Tommy plays it strictly diatonic with regards to note choice in the theme.

The final chord in measure 8, D♭7♯11, which functions as a *tritone substitution* for G7, resolves via half step down to Cmaj7 to kick off another phrase. After briefly tonicizing the Em7 of measure 10 via a ii°–V on beats 3 and 4 of measure 9, an A9 harmony (V/V) resolves as it should to the V chord (D–Dsus4–D(♭5)–D5) in measure 11. Measures 12 and 13 round out the odd, five-measure phrase with F9–F13–Am9. Interestingly, Emmanuel plays essentially the same melody in measures 9–10 over the Cmaj7–F♯m7♭5–B7♯5–Em7 chords as he did in measures 1–2 over the Gmaj7–Am7–Bm7 chords. This is a technique known as *reharmonization*, and it's a great way, as demonstrated here, to make the same melodic material sound fresh again. In measure 11, Gtrs. 1 and 2 come together to sound out a double-stop line that pits chromatically ascending notes on string 2 (F♯–G–G♯–A) against a static D pedal tone on string 1. He caps off the phrase at the end of measure 13 with an ascending sextuplet run up the E blues scale (with an added F♯). Note that this is played over an Am9 chord. This practice of playing a minor pentatonic (or blues scale) off the 5th of a minor chord is a common substitution in jazz.

This entire form essentially repeats, with Emmanuel offering slight variations. Notice, however, that he does extend the form by two extra measures on the repeat. Measure 27 again moves to F13, over which Emmanuel pounds out the 13th (D) in thirty-second-note octaves before descending scale-wise in thirty-second notes on beat 4. He finishes off measure 28 over the Am9–D11 with a 3rds sequence (beat 2) and scalar descent (beat 3).

Fig. 32

* Chord symbols reflect overall harmony.

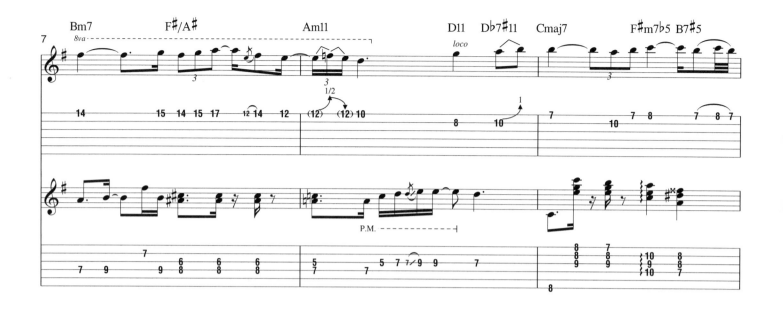

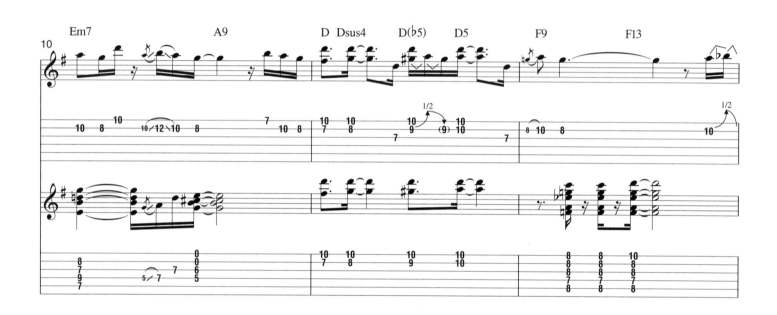

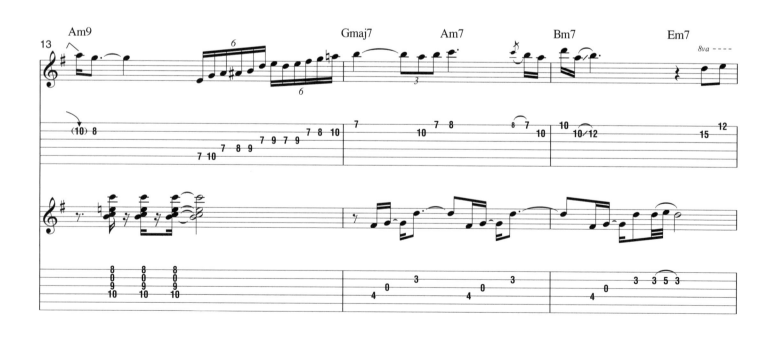

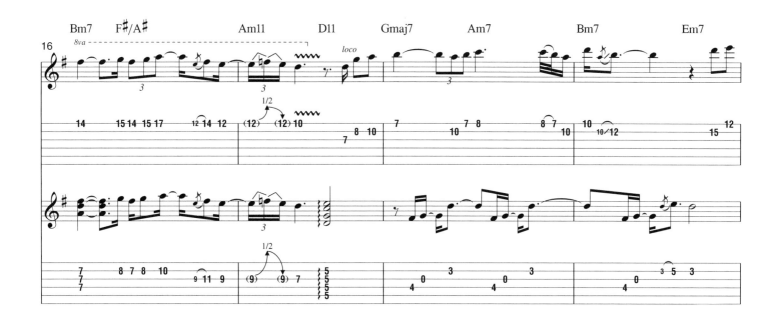

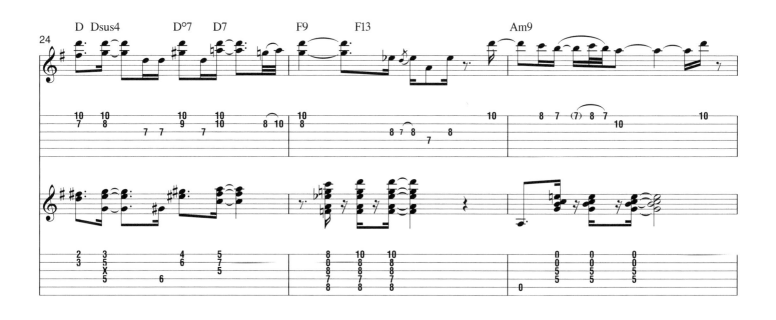

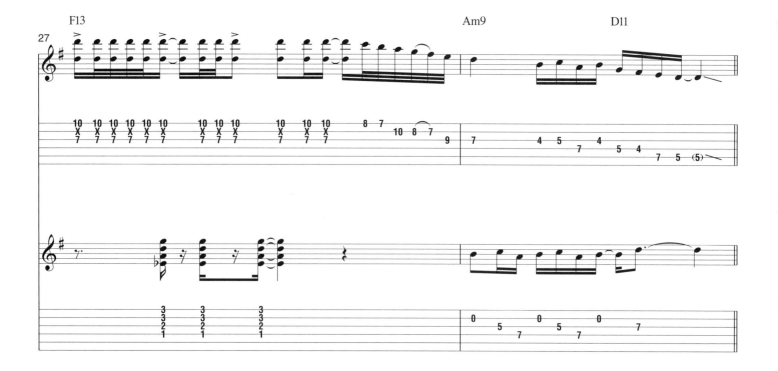

Figure 33—Section ☐D (Guitar Solo)

Emmanuel takes a 13-measure acoustic solo over the changes from the main theme. He begins with sparse statements in measures 1–4, always conscious of the chords over which he's playing. Evidence of this is found in the Bm7 lick that begins at the end of measure 2 and extends halfway through beat 3, which is directly out of the B minor pentatonic box in 7th position. He treats the D11 chord in measure 4 as an *altered dominant*, nicking the ♯9 (spelled enharmonically as F♮) and ♭9 (E♭) just before resolving back to the 5th (D) of the I chord in measure 5.

That D note in measure 5 begins a series of *melodic imitation*, in which he targets the 5th and 3rd of the Gmaj7 (D and B, respectively) and Am7 chords (E and C, respectively). This idea is even extended to the Bm7 chord of measure 6, though the 3rd (D) is delayed until after the 4th (E) sounds. In measure 8, Emmanuel peels off a great "popcorn lick"—one that's not necessarily grounded in theory as much as based off some intervallic or melodic trick or sequence. In this case, he begins by anticipating the V chord by a beat and pecking out the major 3rd interval F♯/D on beat 2. He moves this down by half steps in sextuplet rhythm. On beat 3, though, he alters the melodic pattern (it's not total popcorn!) while maintaining the same rhythm, beginning on a D note and descending chromatically by *minor* 3rds. These subtle adjustments pair critical chord tones with downbeats, lending the lick a good bit more harmonic foundation than if ignored. Again, a lick like this is most effective when you land on your feet, and Emmanuel doesn't miss a beat, outlining the D♭7 on beat 4 with B (C♭ spelled enharmonically) and G—the ♭7th and ♭5th, respectively—before careening through a C major scalar line over the Cmaj7 in measure 9.

He carefully nails the 3rd (D♯) of B7 on beat 4 of measure 9 before bending and sliding around the E minor pentatonic scale to handle the Em7 and A9 changes in measure 10. In measure 11, over the V chord, he peels off a repeated Cmaj7 arpeggio figure, creating a D11 sound—another common substituting device in jazz. Notice how he defines the F13 harmony in measure 12 with the E♭ note before pulling off repeatedly from the 5th (C) to the 9th (G) to bring things to pointed closure.

Fig. 33

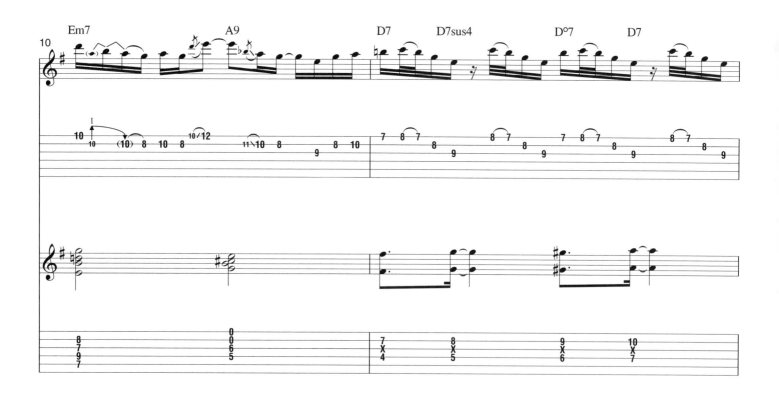

Figure 34—Section F (Outro-Guitar Solo)

For the outro, the harmony consists of a one-chord vamp on Am9. In acknowledgment of this new tonal center, Emmanuel bases his lines almost exclusively on the A minor hexatonic scale (A–B–C–D–E–G) and the A blues scale (A–C–D–Eb–E–G). It seems as though he's ready to release some pent-up energy here, and he wastes no time doing so, unleashing a descending, thirty-second-note pentatonic pattern lick in fifth position that spans two full octaves before you even realize what's hit you. In measure 5, he makes use of rhythmic imitation with a double-stop line, climbing up through the ranks of the Am hexatonic scale before getting gritty with the A blues scale in measure 6. In measure 8, the syncopated, non-adjacent double-stop riff can be seen as derived from the A hexatonic/blues hybrid scale.

More ascending double stops appear in measure 10, climbing all the way up to twelfth position on the high E string, where Emmanuel rips a thirty-second-note pentatonic pull-off lick that climaxes with a high A note all the way up to fret 17 of the high E string—usually uncharted territory on an acoustic guitar. He makes his way back down to seventh position via the hexatonic/blues hybrid scale again before letting loose once more with a furious, alternate-picked line mixing fretted notes in fifth position with the open G string.

Fig. 34

F

62 Full Band

63 Slow Demo
Gtr. 3 meas. 4,
6-7, 11, 13

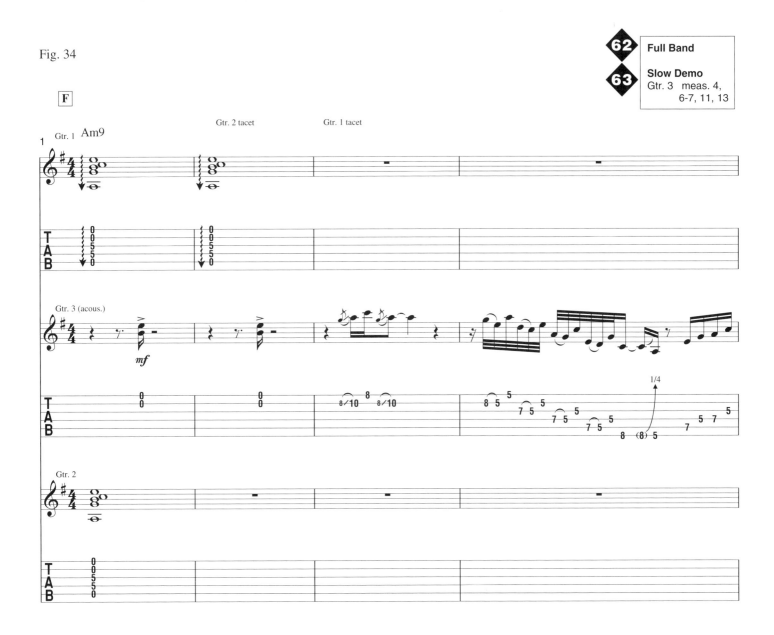

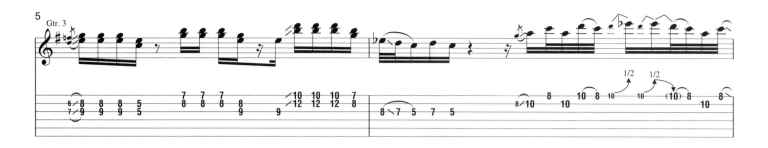

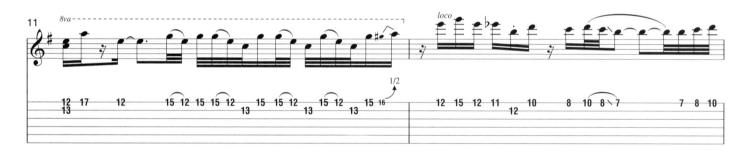

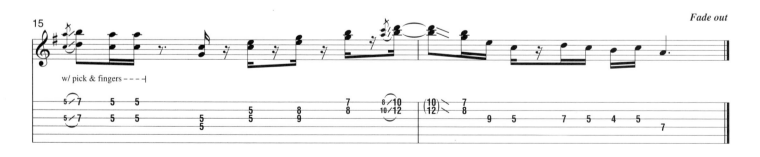

WHO DARES WINS
(*Determination*, 1992)

By Tommy Emmanuel

The final song we'll examine in this volume is "Who Dares Wins" from *Determination*. Tommy operates exclusively on electric for this one, similarly to "From the Hip." A moderate, bouncy shuffle, "Who Dares Wins" is, as a composition, at times reminiscent of the late, great Shawn Lane's work on *Powers of Ten*. With hip, deceptively complex (at times) changes, it allows Emmanuel plenty of opportunity to flex his melodic muscles.

Figure 35—Section C (Theme)

"Who Dares Wins" begins with a long, keyboard-based intro (not shown) that eventually yields to a mellow statement of the main theme on clean-tone electric. Since he plays very nearly the same thing, I've decided to omit that theme and pick it up from section C, which is a full-blown statement complete with a sweet, singing distorted tone on Tommy's part. The Mixolydian changes of G–Gsus4/F lay the harmonic foundation for the first eight-measure phrase. Emmanuel targets a high D (5th) over the G chord and C and G over the Gsus4/F, connecting the two via a soaring bend from C to D. The reiteration of this bend (measures 6–7) climbs up into the stratosphere on account of Emmanuel's use of a harp harmonic created by lightly touching the string (at approx. fret 25) with his right-hand index finger and picking the string directly behind it. The result is a note one octave higher than the fretted note.

In measure 9, he begins to move away from the key of G with a transitional melody that will eventually lead us to section D. Working through Dm–C–A7sus4 changes, Emmanuel targets the ♭3rd (F) of Dm with a half-step bend from E and decorates the C chord with an intervallic, arpeggio-based line. After several bends from C to D (the 9th of C), he lands definitively on the root of A7sus4 in measure 13, sustaining and vibratoing into measure 14. At this point, the key center is a bit ambiguous, but we definitely sense that we're moving somewhere.

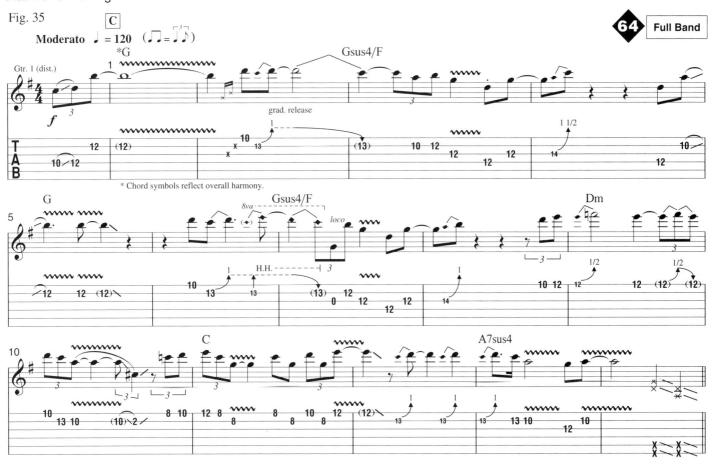

Fig. 35

Figure 36—Section D **(Bridge)**

In section D, Emmanuel and company spin out an angular, syncopated melody comprised mostly of triplets. The harmonies B♭ and C/B♭ suggest a B♭ *Lydian* flavor, and Emmanuel is not shy at all about highlighting the colorful ♯11th (E) over the B♭ bass note. It's at this point that we begin to gain a sense of a home key again, and by measures 3 (F) and 4 (Dm), we can infer that we're in D minor. In fact, when Emmanuel reaches the new tonic (Dm) in measure 4, he lays into a bluesy, pentatonic lick as if to confirm this.

Note the subtle tweaking of the melody in measure 1 for use in measure 3 over the F/A chord. Only two notes have been changed, but they're all that's needed to convey the new harmony. The section closes out with a rise up to the consonant 3rd (A) of F/A in measure 7, to which Emmanuel adds a liberal dose of vibrato.

Fig. 36

65 Full Band

66 Slow Demo
Gtr. 1 meas. 1–4

Figure 37—Section F **(Guitar Solo)**

For the guitar solo, Emmanuel returns to the key of G major, but we have a new set of changes that mixes harmony from G major and the parallel G minor. He opens up with a bit of over-the-bar phrasing, holding a C note (bent a half-step up from B) over the beginning of the G chord for a bit of tension that's quickly resolved in measure 1. He doesn't get to settle into his new home key for long, though, as the E♭/F–B♭/F changes show up in measure 3. Emmanuel is more than ready, and he slides ever-so-smoothly from the final D note in measure 2 up a half step to E♭, as if immediately comfortable in his new surroundings.

He treats the G chords of measures 5–6 with blues licks, beginning with minor pentatonic, shifting to major pentatonic for the climb up to the higher octave, and jumping right back into minor pentatonic for the tasty whole-step bend of B♭ to C. The effect is quite similar to a phrase in Angus Young's "Shook Me All Night Long" solo. Measures 7–8 find Emmanuel pecking at the common G note from a whole step below and a 5th above before gracefully leaping up into the stratosphere range in measure 9. In measure 13, Emmanuel again bluesifies the G chord before settling into a major-sounding double-stop riff in measure 14. Without pausing to think for even a second, he mutates this riff into a descending pattern with recalculated intervals to fit the parallel G minor tonality of measures 15–16. Go T.E.!

Fig. 37

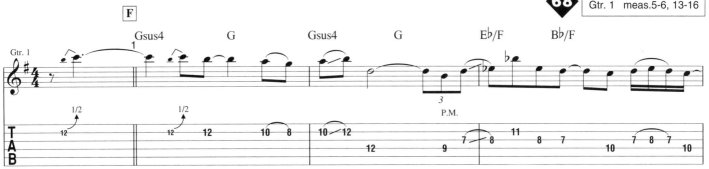

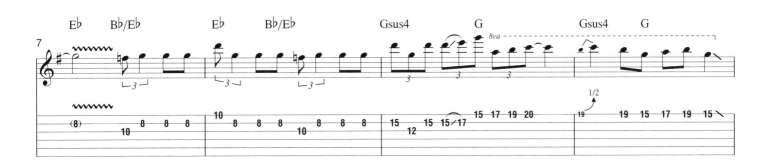

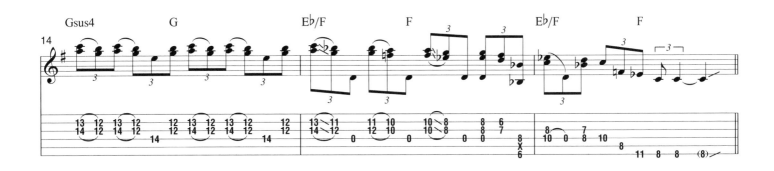

Guitar Notation Legend

Guitar music can be notated three different ways: on a *musical staff*, in *tablature*, and in *rhythm slashes*.

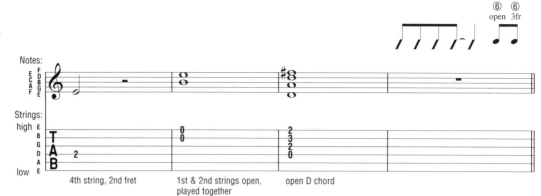

RHYTHM SLASHES are written above the staff. Strum chords in the rhythm indicated. Use the chord diagrams found at the top of the first page of the transcription for the appropriate chord voicings. Round noteheads indicate single notes.

THE MUSICAL STAFF shows pitches and rhythms and is divided by bar lines into measures. Pitches are named after the first seven letters of the alphabet.

TABLATURE graphically represents the guitar fingerboard. Each horizontal line represents a string, and each number represents a fret.

HALF-STEP BEND: Strike the note and bend up 1/2 step.

BEND AND RELEASE: Strike the note and bend up as indicated, then release back to the original note. Only the first note is struck.

HAMMER-ON: Strike the first (lower) note with one finger, then sound the higher note (on the same string) with another finger by fretting it without picking.

TRILL: Very rapidly alternate between the notes indicated by continuously hammering on and pulling off.

PICK SCRAPE: The edge of the pick is rubbed down (or up) the string, producing a scratchy sound.

TREMOLO PICKING: The note is picked as rapidly and continuously as possible.

WHOLE-STEP BEND: Strike the note and bend up one step.

PRE-BEND: Bend the note as indicated, then strike it.

PULL-OFF: Place both fingers on the notes to be sounded. Strike the first note and without picking, pull the finger off to sound the second (lower) note.

TAPPING: Hammer ("tap") the fret indicated with the pick-hand index or middle finger and pull off to the note fretted by the fret hand.

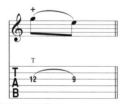

MUFFLED STRINGS: A percussive sound is produced by laying the fret hand across the string(s) without depressing, and striking them with the pick hand.

VIBRATO BAR DIVE AND RETURN: The pitch of the note or chord is dropped a specified number of steps (in rhythm), then returned to the original pitch.

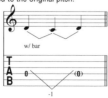

GRACE NOTE BEND: Strike the note and immediately bend up as indicated.

VIBRATO: The string is vibrated by rapidly bending and releasing the note with the fretting hand.

LEGATO SLIDE: Strike the first note and then slide the same fret-hand finger up or down to the second note. The second note is not struck.

NATURAL HARMONIC: Strike the note while the fret-hand lightly touches the string directly over the fret indicated.

PALM MUTING: The note is partially muted by the pick hand lightly touching the string(s) just before the bridge.

VIBRATO BAR SCOOP: Depress the bar just before striking the note, then quickly release the bar.

SLIGHT (MICROTONE) BEND: Strike the note and bend up 1/4 step.

WIDE VIBRATO: The pitch is varied to a greater degree by vibrating with the fretting hand.

SHIFT SLIDE: Same as legato slide, except the second note is struck.

PINCH HARMONIC: The note is fretted normally and a harmonic is produced by adding the edge of the thumb or the tip of the index finger of the pick hand to the normal pick attack.

RAKE: Drag the pick across the strings indicated with a single motion.

VIBRATO BAR DIP: Strike the note and then immediately drop a specified number of steps, then release back to the original pitch.

GUITAR *signature licks*

Signature Licks book/CD packs provide a step-by-step breakdown of "right from the record" riffs, licks, and solos so you can jam along with your favorite bands. They contain performance notes and an overview of each artist's or group's style, with note-for-note transcriptions in notes and tab. The CDs feature full-band demos at both normal and slow speeds.

ACOUSTIC CLASSICS
00695864 ....$19.95

AEROSMITH 1973-1979
00695106 ....$22.95

AEROSMITH 1979-1998
00695219 ....$22.95

BEST OF AGGRO-METAL
00695592 ....$19.95

DUANE ALLMAN
00696042 ....$22.95

BEST OF CHET ATKINS
00695752 ....$22.95

**THE BEACH BOYS
DEFINITIVE COLLECTION**
00695683 ....$22.95

**BEST OF THE BEATLES FOR
ACOUSTIC GUITAR**
00695453 ....$22.95

THE BEATLES BASS
00695283 ....$22.95

THE BEATLES FAVORITES
00695096 ....$24.95

THE BEATLES HITS
00695049 ....$24.95

BEST OF GEORGE BENSON
00695418 ....$22.95

BEST OF BLACK SABBATH
00695249 ....$22.95

BEST OF BLINK - 182
00695704 ....$22.95

BEST OF BLUES GUITAR
00695846 ....$19.95

BLUES GUITAR CLASSICS
00695177 ....$19.95

BLUES/ROCK GUITAR MASTERS
00695348 ....$21.95

KENNY BURRELL
00695830 ....$22.99

BEST OF CHARLIE CHRISTIAN
00695584 ....$22.95

BEST OF ERIC CLAPTON
00695038 ....$24.95

**ERIC CLAPTON –
THE BLUESMAN**
00695040 ....$22.95

**ERIC CLAPTON –
FROM THE ALBUM UNPLUGGED**
00695250 ....$24.95

BEST OF CREAM
00695251 ....$22.95

**CREEDANCE
CLEARWATER REVIVAL**
00695924 ....$22.95

DEEP PURPLE – GREATEST HITS
00695625 ....$22.95

THE BEST OF DEF LEPPARD
00696516 ....$22.95

THE DOORS
00695373 ....$22.95

ESSENTIAL JAZZ GUITAR
00695875 ....$19.99

FAMOUS ROCK GUITAR SOLOS
00695590 ....$19.95

BEST OF FOO FIGHTERS
00695481 ....$24.95

ROBBEN FORD
00695903 ....$22.95

**GREATEST GUITAR SOLOS
OF ALL TIME**
00695301 ....$19.95

BEST OF GRANT GREEN
00695747 ....$22.95

BEST OF GUNS N' ROSES
00695183 ....$24.95

THE BEST OF BUDDY GUY
00695186 ....$22.95

JIM HALL
00695848 ....$22.99

HARD ROCK SOLOS
00695591 ....$19.95

JIMI HENDRIX
00696560 ....$24.95

JIMI HENDRIX – VOLUME 2
00695835 ....$24.95

JOHN LEE HOOKER
00695894 ....$19.99

HOT COUNTRY GUITAR
00695580 ....$19.95

BEST OF JAZZ GUITAR
00695586 ....$24.95

ERIC JOHNSON
00699317 ....$24.95

ROBERT JOHNSON
00695264 ....$22.95

BARNEY KESSEL
00696009 ....$22.99

THE ESSENTIAL ALBERT KING
00695713 ....$22.95

**B.B. KING –
THE DEFINITIVE COLLECTION**
00695635 ....$22.95

B.B. KING – MASTER BLUESMAN
00699923 ....$24.99

THE KINKS
00695553 ....$22.95

BEST OF KISS
00699413 ....$22.95

MARK KNOPFLER
00695178 ....$22.95

LYNYRD SKYNYRD
00695872 ....$24.95

BEST OF YNGWIE MALMSTEEN
00695669 ....$22.95

BEST OF PAT MARTINO
00695632 ....$24.99

WES MONTGOMERY
00695387 ....$24.95

BEST OF NIRVANA
00695483 ....$24.95

THE OFFSPRING
00695852 ....$24.95

VERY BEST OF OZZY OSBOURNE
00695431 ....$22.95

BEST OF JOE PASS
00695730 ....$22.95

TOM PETTY
00696021 ....$22.99

PINK FLOYD – EARLY CLASSICS
00695566 ....$22.95

THE POLICE
00695724 ....$22.95

THE GUITARS OF ELVIS
00696507 ....$22.95

BEST OF QUEEN
00695097 ....$24.95

**BEST OF
RAGE AGAINST THE MACHINE**
00695480 ....$24.95

RED HOT CHILI PEPPERS
00695173 ....$22.95

**RED HOT CHILI PEPPERS –
GREATEST HITS**
00695828 ....$24.95

BEST OF DJANGO REINHARDT
00695660 ....$24.95

BEST OF ROCK
00695884 ....$19.95

BEST OF ROCK 'N' ROLL GUITAR
00695559 ....$19.95

BEST OF ROCKABILLY GUITAR
00695785 ....$19.95

THE ROLLING STONES
00695079 ....$24.95

BEST OF DAVID LEE ROTH
00695843 ....$24.95

BEST OF JOE SATRIANI
00695216 ....$22.95

BEST OF SILVERCHAIR
00695488 ....$22.95

THE BEST OF SOUL GUITAR
00695703 ....$19.95

BEST OF SOUTHERN ROCK
00695560 ....$19.95

MIKE STERN
00695800 ....$24.99

ROD STEWART
00695663 ....$22.95

BEST OF SURF GUITAR
00695822 ....$19.95

BEST OF SYSTEM OF A DOWN
00695788 ....$22.95

ROCK BAND
00696063 ....$22.99

ROBIN TROWER
00695950 ....$22.95

STEVE VAI
00673247 ....$22.95

**STEVE VAI – ALIEN LOVE
SECRETS: THE NAKED VAMPS**
00695223 ....$22.95

**STEVE VAI – FIRE GARDEN:
THE NAKED VAMPS**
00695166 ....$22.95

**STEVE VAI – THE ULTRA ZONE:
NAKED VAMPS**
00695684 ....$22.95

STEVIE RAY VAUGHAN – 2ND ED.
00699316 ....$24.95

**THE GUITAR STYLE OF
STEVIE RAY VAUGHAN**
00695155 ....$24.95

BEST OF THE VENTURES
00695772 ....$19.95

THE WHO – 2ND ED.
00695561 ....$22.95

JOHNNY WINTER
00695951 ....$22.99

BEST OF ZZ TOP
00695738 ....$24.95

FOR MORE INFORMATION,
SEE YOUR LOCAL MUSIC DEALER,
OR WRITE TO:

HAL•LEONARD®
CORPORATION
7777 W. BLUEMOUND RD. P.O. BOX 13819
MILWAUKEE, WISCONSIN 53213

www.halleonard.com

COMPLETE DESCRIPTIONS AND SONGLISTS ONLINE!
Prices, contents and availability subject to change without notice.

0410

RECORDED VERSIONS®

The Best Note-For-Note Transcriptions Available

ALL BOOKS INCLUDE TABLATURE

00692015 Aerosmith – Greatest Hits $22.95	00690841 Scott Henderson – Blues Guitar Collection ..$19.95	00690670 Queensryche – Very Best of $19.95
00690178 Alice in Chains – Acoustic.......................$19.95	00692930 Jimi Hendrix – Are You Experienced?..........$24.95	00690878 The Raconteurs – Broken Boy Soldiers $19.95
00694865 Alice in Chains – Dirt..............................$19.95	00692931 Jimi Hendrix – Axis: Bold As Love.............$22.95	00694910 Rage Against the Machine $19.95
00690812 All American Rejects – Move Along.............$19.95	00692932 Jimi Hendrix – Electric Ladyland $24.95	00690055 Red Hot Chili Peppers –
00690958 Duane Allman Guitar Anthology $24.99	00690017 Jimi Hendrix – Live at Woodstock...............$24.95	Blood Sugar Sex Magik.............................$19.95
00694932 Allman Brothers Band – Volume 1 ....$24.95	00690602 Jimi Hendrix – Smash Hits.........................$24.99	00690584 Red Hot Chili Peppers – By the Way.............$19.95
00694933 Allman Brothers Band – Volume 2 ....$24.95	00690793 John Lee Hooker Anthology $24.99	00690852 Red Hot Chili Peppers –Stadium Arcadium ..$24.95
00694934 Allman Brothers Band – Volume 3 ....$24.95	00690692 Billy Idol – Very Best of $19.95	00690511 Django Reinhardt – Definitive Collection $19.95
00690865 Atreyu – A Deathgrip on Yesterday $19.95	00690688 Incubus – A Crow Left of the Murder............$19.95	00690779 Relient K – MMHMM..............................$19.95
00690609 Audioslave $19.95	00690544 Incubus – Morningview..............................$19.95	00690631 Rolling Stones – Guitar Anthology................$27.95
00690820 Avenged Sevenfold – City of Evil $24.95	00690790 Iron Maiden Anthology $24.99	00694976 Rolling Stones – Some Girls $22.95
00690366 Bad Company – Original Anthology $19.95	00690721 Jet – Get Born...$19.95	00690264 The Rolling Stones – Tattoo You $19.95
00690503 Beach Boys – Very Best of $19.95	00690684 Jethro Tull – Aqualung...............................$19.95	00690685 David Lee Roth – Eat 'Em and Smile $19.95
00690489 Beatles – 1 ....$24.99	00690959 John5 – Requiem $22.95	00690942 David Lee Roth and the Songs of Van Halen .$19.95
00694832 Beatles – For Acoustic Guitar $22.99	00690814 John5 – Songs for Sanity $19.95	00690031 Santana's Greatest Hits $19.95
00691014 Beatles Rock Band $34.99	00690751 John5 – Vertigo $19.95	00690566 Scorpions – Best of $22.95
00690110 Beatles – White Album (Book 1) $19.95	00690845 Eric Johnson – Bloom $19.95	00690604 Bob Seger – Guitar Collection....................$19.95
00692385 Chuck Berry $19.95	00690846 Jack Johnson and Friends – Sing-A-Longs and	00690803 Kenny Wayne Shepherd Band – Best of........$19.95
00690835 Billy Talent $19.95	Lullabies for the Film Curious George $19.95	00690968 Shinedown – The Sound of Madness $22.99
00690901 Best of Black Sabbath $19.95	00690271 Robert Johnson – New Transcriptions $24.95	00690813 Slayer – Guitar Collection..........................$19.95
00690831 blink-182 – Greatest Hits $19.95	00699131 Janis Joplin – Best of $19.95	00690530 Slipknot – Iowa $19.95
00690913 Boston $19.95	00690427 Judas Priest – Best of................................$22.99	00690733 Slipknot – Vol. 3 (The Subliminal Verses) $22.99
00690932 Boston – Don't Look Back $19.99	00690742 The Killers – Hot Fuss..............................$19.95	00120004 Steely Dan – Best of..................................$24.95
00690491 David Bowie – Best of...............................$19.95	00690975 Kings of Leon – Only by the Night $22.99	00694921 Steppenwolf – Best of................................$22.95
00690873 Breaking Benjamin – Phobia $19.95	00694903 Kiss – Best of..$24.95	00690655 Mike Stern – Best of $19.95
00690451 Jeff Buckley – Collection............................$24.95	00690355 Kiss – Destroyer $16.95	00690877 Stone Sour – Come What(ever) May $19.95
00690957 Bullet for My Valentine – Scream Aim Fire....$19.95	00690930 Korn $19.95	00690520 Styx Guitar Collection................................$19.95
00691004 Chickenfoot $22.99	00690834 Lamb of God – Ashes of the Wake $19.95	00120081 Sublime $19.95
00690590 Eric Clapton – Anthology $29.95	00690875 Lamb of God – Sacrament $19.95	00120122 Sublime – 40oz. to Freedom $19.95
00690415 Clapton Chronicles – Best of Eric Clapton.....$18.95	00690823 Ray LaMontagne – Trouble $19.95	00690929 Sum 41 – Underclass Hero $19.95
00690936 Eric Clapton – Complete Clapton $29.99	00690679 John Lennon – Guitar Collection................$19.95	00690767 Switchfoot – The Beautiful Letdown............$19.95
00690074 Eric Clapton – The Cream of Clapton...........$24.95	00690781 Linkin Park – Hybrid Theory $22.95	00690993 Taylor Swift – Fearless $22.99
00694869 Eric Clapton – Unplugged $22.95	00690743 Los Lonely Boys $19.95	00690830 System of a Down – Hypnotize $19.95
00690162 The Clash – Best of..................................$19.95	00690720 Lostprophets – Start Something $19.95	00690799 System of a Down – Mezmerize $19.95
00690828 Coheed & Cambria – Good Apollo I'm	00690955 Lynyrd Skynyrd – All-Time Greatest Hits $19.99	00690531 System of a Down – Toxicity $19.95
Burning Star, IV, Vol. 1: From Fear	00694954 Lynyrd Skynyrd – New Best of.....................$19.95	00694824 James Taylor – Best of...............................$16.95
Through the Eyes of Madness $19.95	00690754 Marilyn Manson – Lest We Forget................$19.95	00690871 Three Days Grace – One-X $19.95
00690593 Coldplay – A Rush of Blood to the Head $19.95	00694956 Bob Marley– Legend.................................$19.95	00690737 3 Doors Down – The Better Life $22.95
00690962 Coldplay – Viva La Vida $19.95	00694945 Bob Marley– Songs of Freedom $24.95	00690683 Robin Trower – Bridge of Sighs $19.95
00690819 Creedence Clearwater Revival – Best of $22.95	00690657 Maroon5 – Songs About Jane $19.95	00699191 U2 – Best of: 1980-1990 ....$19.95
00690648 The Very Best of Jim Croce $19.95	00120080 Don McLean – Songbook $19.95	00690732 U2 – Best of: 1990-2000 ....$19.95
00690613 Crosby, Stills & Nash – Best of $22.95	00694951 Megadeth – Rust in Peace $22.95	00660137 Steve Vai – Passion & Warfare....................$24.95
00690967 Death Cab for Cutie – Narrow Stairs $22.99	00690951 Megadeth – United Abominations $22.99	00690116 Stevie Ray Vaughan – Guitar Collection........$24.95
00690289 Deep Purple – Best of...............................$17.95	00690505 John Mellencamp – Guitar Collection...........$19.95	00660058 Stevie Ray Vaughan –
00690784 Def Leppard – Best of $19.95	00690646 Pat Metheny – One Quiet Night $19.95	Lightnin' Blues 1983-1987......................$24.95
00692240 Bo Diddley $19.99	00690558 Pat Metheny – Trio: 99>00........................$19.95	00694835 Stevie Ray Vaughan – The Sky Is Crying $22.95
00690347 The Doors – Anthology...............................$22.95	00690040 Steve Miller Band – Young Hearts................$19.95	00690015 Stevie Ray Vaughan – Texas Flood...............$19.95
00690348 The Doors – Essential Guitar Collection.........$16.95	00694883 Nirvana – Nevermind...............................$19.95	00690772 Velvet Revolver – Contraband $22.95
00690810 Fall Out Boy – From Under the Cork Tree.....$19.95	00690026 Nirvana – Unplugged in New York $19.95	00690071 Weezer (The Blue Album) $19.95
00690664 Fleetwood Mac – Best of............................$19.95	00690807 The Offspring – Greatest Hits....................$19.95	00690966 Weezer – (Red Album) $19.99
00690870 Flyleaf $19.95	00694847 Ozzy Osbourne – Best of............................$22.95	00690447 The Who – Best of...................................$24.95
00690931 Foo Fighters – Echoes, Silence,	00690399 Ozzy Osbourne – Ozzman Cometh $19.95	00690916 The Best of Dwight Yoakam $19.95
Patience & Grace $19.95	00690933 Best of Brad Paisley $22.95	00690905 Neil Young – Rust Never Sleeps $19.99
00690808 Foo Fighters – In Your Honor $19.95	00690995 Brad Paisley – Play: The Guitar Album $24.99	00690623 Frank Zappa – Over-Nite Sensation $19.95
00690805 Robben Ford – Best of...............................$19.95	00690866 Panic! At the Disco –	00690589 ZZ Top Guitar Anthology.............................$24.95
00694920 Free – Best of $19.95	A Fever You Can't Sweat Out $19.95	
00690848 Godsmack – IV..$19.95	00690938 Christopher Parkening –	
00690601 Good Charlotte –	Duets & Concertos $24.99	
The Young and the Hopeless......................$19.95	00694855 Pearl Jam – Ten.......................................$19.95	
00690943 The Goo Goo Dolls – Greatest Hits	00690439 A Perfect Circle – Mer De Noms $19.95	
Volume 1: The Singles $22.95	00690499 Tom Petty – Definitive Guitar Collection........$19.95	
00694854 Buddy Guy – Damn Right,	00690428 Pink Floyd – Dark Side of the Moon $19.95	
I've Got the Blues $19.95	00690789 Poison – Best of.......................................$19.95	
00690840 Ben Harper – Both Sides of the Gun $19.95	00693864 The Police – Best of..................................$19.95	
00694798 George Harrison – Anthology $19.95	00694975 Queen – Greatest Hits...............................$24.95	

Prices and availability subject to change without notice. Some products may not be available outside the U.S.A.